AF838122

# The Design and Human Environment Learning and Style Guide

Third Edition

Elaine L. Pedersen
*Oregon State University*

Kendall Hunt
publishing company

Kendall Hunt
publishing company

www.kendallhunt.com
*Send all inquiries to:*
4050 Westmark Drive
Dubuque, IA 52004-1840



ISBN 978-1-4652-4038-5



Printed in the United States of America
10 9 8 7 6 5 4 3 2 1

# Contents

# Preface

The purpose of this guide is to help you improve your learning and performance. Scholars have identified styles of learning, and, if you are familiar with your style of learning, you can design your note-taking and other study skills to fit your learning style. A quiz located in Chapter One will help you identify your learning style(s). Additionally, tips to use for reading your assignments and taking essay exams are provided in the first chapter.

Poor communication is often a source of confusion between students and instructors. In the second chapter, commonly used assignment and exam terms are discussed and defined along with what DHE instructors expect when these terms are utilized.

Academic disciplines have specific documentation styles for the presentation and format of formal papers.[1] Using a shared style makes it possible for papers produced in each academic area to present ideas in a standard format. The style that is most commonly used in DHE-related publications and which is required for undergraduate and graduate student papers in DHE is the American Psychological Association (APA) style. Those aspects of the APA style that are important for papers, as well as comments designed to help you improve your papers, are discussed in the third chapter.

The final section of the handbook is designed as a guide to help you evaluate print and Web resources. With the increase in information availability in the last several decades, it is important to be able to identify the differences between useful resources and those that are unreliable or have other problems.

I would like to thank the faculty of the School of Design and Human Environment at Oregon State University for all of their support over the years. Without their suggestions for development and revisions, the style guide would not exist today.

## *Endnote*

1. Formal papers, such as term papers, are different from informal papers (e.g., in-class writing assignments, journals, etc.).

CHAPTER ONE

# Styles of Learning and Learning Tips

Researchers have found that the most successful students are those who accept the responsibility for their learning. These students set realistic but challenging goals. Students who become frustrated may have set their goals too high, may have unrealistic goals, or may not have set goals. Successful learners know what their learning styles are. They have discovered that they learn successfully in certain environments (e.g., alone or with friends, with music, or with minimal sound interference, etc.). They have also learned how to be successful note-takers and test-takers, along with having developed the skills to complete class projects. Successful learners are also not shy about asking the instructor for help or advice. Additionally, successful learners understand, at least partially, why what they are studying is and will be important in their future—whether in their personal or professional lives (Weinstein, 1994).

While there is much agreement that individuals have a variety of learning styles, many different types of learning styles have been identified. Some scholars identify learning styles by type (i.e., visual, aural, and so forth) while other scholars see learning styles as a combination of different dimensions (Felder & Soloman, n.d.; Fleming & Mills, 1992).

Four styles of learning have been identified by Neil D. Fleming and Colleen Mills (1992). They are visual, aural, reading/writing, and kinesthetic. If an individual learns only or primarily with one of these styles of learning, particular study skills will be best suited to that one learning style. If an individual learns with several styles of learning, then a broader range of study skills will be best suited to her/him. Fleming and Mills take the approach that different learning styles (or combinations of learning styles) work for different individuals. Take the "Learning" test below to determine what type of learning style(s) fits you best (according to Fleming and Mills, 1992).

## How Do I Learn Best?

The test below has been designed by Fleming and Mills (1992) to help you discover your preferred learning method. Researchers have learned that every individual has a preferred learning orientation; we all convey and receive information in different ways.

Select the answer that is closest to your preference; select several answers when they fit your preference best. Don't force a choice; instead, leave a question blank if it doesn't apply.

1. You are about to give directions to a person. She is staying in a hotel in town and wants to visit your house. She has a rental car. Would you:

   V) draw a map on paper?
   A) tell her the directions?
   R) write down the directions (without a map)?
   K) collect her from the hotel in your car?

2. You are staying in a hotel and have a rental car. You would like to visit a friend whose address/location you do not know. Would you like them to:

   V) draw you a map on paper?
   A) tell you the directions?
   R) write down the directions (without a map)?
   K) collect you from the hotel in your car?

3. You have just received a copy of your itinerary for a world trip. This is of interest to a friend. Would you:

   A) call her immediately and tell her about it?
   R) send her a copy of the printed itinerary?
   V) show her a map of the world?

4. You are going to cook a dessert as a special treat for your family. Do you:

   K) cook something familiar without need for instructions?
   V) thumb through the cookbook for ideas from the pictures?
   R) refer to a specific cookbook where there is a good recipe?
   A) ask for advice from others?

5. A group of tourists has been assigned to you to find out about national parks. Would you:

   K) drive them to a national park?
   V) show them slides and photographs?
   R) give them a book on national parks?
   A) give them a talk on national parks?

6. You are about to purchase a new stereo. Other than price, what would most influence your decision?

   A) a friend talking about it
   R) reading the details about it
   K) listening to it
   V) its distinctive, upscale appearance

7. Recall a time in your life when you learned how to do something like playing a new board game. Try to avoid choosing a very physical skill (e.g., riding a bike). How did you learn best? By:

   V) visual clues: pictures, diagrams, charts?
   A) listening to somebody explaining it?
   K) doing it?
   R) written instructions?

8. Which of these games do you prefer?

   V) Pictionary
   R) Scrabble
   K) Charades

9. You are about to learn to use a new program on a computer. Would you:

   K) ask a friend to show you?
   R) read the manual which comes with the program?
   A) telephone a friend and ask questions about it?

10. You are not sure whether a word should be spelled 'dependent' or 'dependant.' Do you:

    R) look it up in the dictionary?
    V) see the word in your mind and choose the best way it looks?
    A) sound it out in your mind?
    K) write both versions down?

11. Apart from price, what would most influence your decision to buy a particular textbook?

    K) using a friend's copy
    A) a friend talking about it
    R) skimming parts of it
    V) it looks OK

12. A new movie has arrived in town. What would most influence your decision to go or not go?

    A) friends talked about it
    R) you read a review about it
    V) you saw a preview of it

13. Do you prefer a lecturer/teacher who likes to use:

    R) handouts and/or a textbook?
    K) field trips, labs, practical sessions?
    V) flow diagrams, charts, slides?
    A) discussion, guest speakers?

Each of the answers in the "Learning" test is labeled with a letter that represents a particular learning style (i.e., V-visual, A-aural, R-reading/writing, & K-kinesthetic). Count how many responses you made for each category (i.e., how many "V's", "A's", "R's", & "K's") to identify your learning style(s). If most answers are in one category, this is your learning style. Answers divided among two or more categories mean you learn with several styles. The Learning Modality table on the following page will help you determine your best approach in class, how to study course material, and how to study for exams. Your best learning will occur if you study regularly.

*TABLE 1*

***Learning Suggestions for Learning Styles*[a]**

| Lecture and Reading Notes | When Studying | Performing Well on Exams |
|---|---|---|
| Visual | | |
| underline | use the techniques in left column | recall the images and symbols |
| use different colors | draw page from memory | draw, use diagrams when appropriate |
| use highlighters | replace words with symbols | turn visuals into words |
| use symbols | close your eyes to remember | |
| make flow charts | avoid distractions | |
| make graphs | learn big picture first | |
| use/make pictures | use flash cards | |
| avoid distractions | | |
| make mind/concept maps | | |
| make flash cards | | |
| Aural | | |
| attend all lectures | expand your notes talking to others | ask questions if you have them |
| record lectures | record and listen to expanded | listen to your voices and write them down |
| explain ideas to others | share your understanding with others | recall your ideas before writing |
| use a recorder | read your expanded notes aloud | speak your answers (quietly) |
| remember interesting examples, stories | discuss your ideas out loud | |
| describe illustrations | | |
| leave space in your notes for expansion | | |
| discuss with others | | |
| read textbooks out loud | | |
| Reading/Writing | | |
| make lists | reduce your notes | write exam answers |
| use headings | write your notes over and over | practice with multiple choice questions |
| use dictionaries | rewrite ideas into other words | write your lists |
| use handouts | organize visuals into words | |
| use textbooks | turn charts into words | |
| use readings | make multiple choice questions | |
| use lecture notes | | |
| Kinesthetic | | |
| use all of your senses | expand your notes to taljing to others | write practice answers |
| go on field trips | use many examples in your notes | role play exam situation |
| create examples of key ideas, principles | talk to another "K" student | |
| use hands-on approach | use illustrations | |
| find examples | recall your examples | |
| be active while studying | take frequent study breaks | |
| chew gum | | |
| work while standing | | |

[a] Modified "Appendix B" from Fleming and Mills (1992, pp. 152–153); additional information from Three Learning Styles (2002–2010) and What's Your Learning Style? (2009)

## Other Learning Styles

As discussed above there are a variety of views on learning styles. The learning style quiz developed by Fleming and Mills (1992) above may not be the best fit for improving your learning. If you go to the World Wide Web and Google "learning styles" you will find a variety of learning style quizzes and learning style strategies. If you are frustrated about your ability to learn material, you may want to spend some time exploring this information.

## Tips for Success in Learning

Make a commitment to yourself. Come to class ready to listen to others and to participate in class activities. Don't try to finish other work in class. Multitasking has been found to be unsuccessful.

Rather than attempting to write down every word of lecture or discussion, experiment with using cue words, key phrases, and so forth. Often one hears and understands at a deeper level with a minimum level of note-taking. But, since everyone learns differently, you must experiment to find the best strategy for yourself. After class, or later in the day, you can fill in your notes. However, do not wait longer than necessary or you may not remember adequately.

Remember that this is your education. "Successful students get involved in their studies, accept responsibility for their own education, and are active participants in it!" ("Successful Students," 1996). Set goals for yourself. Don't hesitate to ask questions of the instructor—in class, during office hours, or via telephone or e-mail. The instructor wants you to learn; she/he wants to be supportive of your learning activities. Sit in the front of the class: there will be fewer distractions. Take good notes. Your notes need to be understandable and organized; review them frequently. If you can learn your subject well enough that you can put it into words, you can be successful in the subject. Don't cram for your examinations (i.e., wait until the night before the exam and then study late into the night); "divided periods of study are more effective than cram session" ("Successful Students," 1996, p. 2). See the Appendix for learning resources available on the Web.

## Tips for Reading Assignments

Prior to reading an assignment, glance at the material and make an outline. Next, look at the outline and ask yourself what you will learn. Ask yourself questions, and answer the questions as you read. Read carefully and recite the answers out loud. When you finish reading, go back to the outline—does it make sense? Cover up the outline and recall the main ideas. Take notes as you read, and highlight key points. Look for the main ideas; do not copy everything (Robinson, 1970). Develop a brief set of questions and then as you read, watch for the answers to the questions.

As you read, take notes and highlight the important points in each paragraph. When you come to words that are new to you, take the time to define them. When you are taking notes do not copy everything. Look for the main points and effective concepts (Robinson, 1970).

## Tips for Preparing for Exams

One of the most effective strategies for learning course materials and performing well on course exams is to begin preparing the first week of classes. Studying early in the term and regularly throughout the term, like exercising regularly, is a very successful means of learning any subject matter. Plan your study times, include study breaks, and keep to your schedule. It is also a good idea to study your most difficult subjects first, when you are fresh. Look at the suggestions above on how to be effective with your reading assignments.

Be an active learner. The more you study and review the material the more you will understand it. If you can develop a variety of methods of studying this will help you retain the information. Review course materials once a week or more often; review both the assigned reading and your lecture notes. Make written summaries of the material that has been covered. If at any time you have questions on the materials, contact your instructor who can help clarify the information or understand a particular process or procedure.

Whenever you study the material (whether reviewing the first chapter, the first week, or the material to be covered on the first exam) begin with an overview. Determine and summarize the main ideas and any supporting data or information. After you have determined the basic ideas then move on to study the details. It has been determined that taking notes is better than underlining, so develop a "meaty" outline of the material. If there are specific kinds of information that need to be memorized make flash cards and then carry them with you and study them throughout each day.

Researchers have found that "overstudying" can be very effective. Study until you believe you know the material and then continue studying for about another quarter of the amount of time you have already used. In other words, if you studied the material for four hours the week before the exam, you would put in another hour of study after you felt you knew the material.

The night before the exam, complete an intensive review of the material. Summarize and make sense of your review materials. You may want to develop a mnemonic device to help you remember lists of information or devices. Judge by what has been effective for you in the past in deciding what type of strategies to use. The suggestions below of different types of mnemonic devices come from the Bucks County Community College Web site on "The Basics of Effective Learning" ("Test-Taking," 2011):

- To help you remember key words, use acronyms or invented combinations of letters. Example: To remember the basic design elements of line, form, space, texture, and color your acronym would be LFSPTC.
- To remember words or ideas, use acrostics or invented sentences using the first letter of each word as a cue to words or ideas. Example: To remember the stages in the fashion process (creation, fashion leadership, increasing social visibility, conformity, saturation, and decline and obsolescence, you could create the following sentence (first letter of words to remember are capitalized): Certainly, Following Ladies Involves Spurning Vamps, Continuing Silence, and Disturbing Others.
- To remember a number of items, names of individuals, and so forth, place each item (or person, etc.) in a specific location in a room well known to you. Example, for early 20th century apparel designers: When I walked into the living room Doucet was looking out the front window while Poiret was in the large, beige chair. Fortuny was examining the CD shelves and Paquin was on the sofa.
- To remember names, create a relationship between the name and the physical (or other) characteristics of the person. Example, to remember Palladio, a 16th century Italian Renaissance architect: Palladio and a temple front.
- To remember lists, make a story where each word or idea you want to remember cues the next idea or word. Example, putting the English kings in chronological order: Henry VIII was the father of Elizabeth I. James I was Elizabeth's cousin while Charles I was James's son. Oliver Cromwell ruled after Charles I was beheaded in the English Civil War, and Charles II, the eldest son of Charles I, ruled after Cromwell. ("Test-Taking," 2011).

The process of developing these mnemonic devices, the writing down of your cues, and the revisiting of your cues as you review your materials will help you remember.

Do not plan on an "all-nighter." Researchers have discovered that trying to cram three or more weeks of knowledge into your head in one night is not effective and not successful.

## Tips for multiple-choice exams

Multiple-choice questions are composed of a stem and up to five possible responses. Responses include the best answer and two to four distractors. Normally there will be only one correct answer. In studying for a multiple-choice exam, follow the general tips for test preparation above.

When taking a multiple-choice exam it is best to use your knowledge to answer the questions. Though there are some clues that may be useful, you cannot always rely on finding those clues or having an instructor that writes "standard" multiple-choice questions.

In answering a multiple choice question, *start by reading the stem and providing your own answer to the stem without looking at the choices.* Rely also on reasoning and reading the stem and the distractors very carefully. Underline key words and terms, if permitted to do so. If the stem is complex, simplify the wording. Look at the choices and think about what each answer is saying; ask yourself if this answer fits the stem. Do not jump to conclusions. Only if you are unable to do this (which means you probably did not begin preparing for the exam early in the term), look at each of the answers and consider the following:

- if an option has always, generally, often, seldom, never, none, except, most, or least this may not be the answer (do remember that sometimes there are exceptions)
- sometimes the correct answer is the longest
- neither of two choices that are very similar will be the answer
- when there are two choices which are opposite in meaning one will be the answer, especially if they contain all possible answers

## Tips for essay exams

In studying for any exam, you should do more than just read or re-read the text and your class notes. Using more than one sense (i.e., eyes, ears, touch—writing) enables you to retain the information better than if you only use one sense. In studying for an essay exam (or in answering questions on a study guide) it is helpful if you write out practice answers—this utilizes the eyes and touch senses. If you also say the information that you are writing out loud, then you are using three of your senses.

When taking the exam, read the question carefully and note key words. For example, if you are asked to "describe" and "discuss" be sure to do both. Before beginning to write your exam answer, do brainstorming on scratch paper or in the margins. You may find it helpful to make a quick outline of the major ideas related to the question. If you have several essay questions in your exam, look at each and write down ideas for each before you begin to write.

When you begin to write your answer(s), begin your answer with a thesis statement[1] and then support what you have said. Be as specific as you can be in your answer and use key terms, phrases, and theories (when relevant). Your strongest points should be in your first and final paragraphs. Use indented paragraphs. This will enable the instructor to see each of your points. Concentrate on your content; you can correct spelling and punctuation when you have answered all of the questions. You do not need to answer all of the questions in order. Answer those you know best first and then answer the remaining question(s) (McKowen, 1996).

# Sample Essay Exam Answers

The following two examples are provided to give you an example of a *passing essay exam* and an *above average essay exam*. The essay question for these two essay exam answers was:

> Discuss the potential role of the material environment and the individual-based production in enhancing individuals' sense of self and quality of life.

Note that the *above average essay exam* answer has greater depth, more explanation, and more examples. Prior to taking an essay exam, check with your instructor to determine what her/his expectations are with regard to the content, length, depth, use of examples, and other items of importance.

## Passing essay exam answer

The material environment and individual-based production can play an important part in enhancing individuals' sense of self and their quality of life. The production process gives the individual a sense of fulfillment and self-confidence. This is particularly true of goods produced by an individual and then shared with family and friends. These products, when given to a significant other, create a bond between the maker/receiver and the owner/receiver.

Items individuals select for their near material environment (the home/office) may have symbolic meaning which adds to the individual's comfort level and enjoyment of their space. Individuals who are interested in the production of items often share this interest with friends or groups of individuals. An example of this sharing process is the guild or club system. There are many different types of these guilds: calligraphy, embroidery, painting, quilting, rug hooking, spinning, weaving, and so forth. Individuals involved in these groups receive many benefits including learning activities resulting in new or increased skills and knowledge and opportunities for making friends and building a support system.

The making of products provides individuals with a sense of self-worth and adds to their quality of life. The sharing of these products with others creates a link between the maker and new owner. When the individual also interacts with others interested in the same production process a support system may develop, providing additional benefits for the individual.

## Above average essay exam answer

The material environment and individual-based production can play an important part in enhancing individuals' sense of self and their quality of life. This is particularly true when there is a link between the material environment and the production process in which the individual is engaged.

The material environment is the tangible component of the world that surrounds the individual. Much of the material environment is human-constructed. Items individuals select for their near material environment (the home/office) may have symbolic meaning which adds to the individual's comfort level and enjoyment of their space.

The production process gives the individual a sense of fulfillment and self-confidence. This is particularly true of goods produced by an individual and then shared with family and friends. When given to significant others, these products create a bond between the maker/receiver and the owner/receiver.

Individuals who are interested in the production of items often share this interest with friends or groups of individuals. An example of this sharing process is the guild or club system. There are many different types of these guilds: calligraphy, embroidery, painting, quilting, rug hooking, spinning, weaving, woodcarving, and so forth. Individuals involved in these groups receive many benefits, including learning activities resulting in new or increased skills and knowledge and opportunities for making friends and building a support system.

An example of the importance of the material environment and individual-based productions can be found with quilt makers and quilts. Quilters utilize quilts to communicate their feelings, and quilts become symbols for the maker and the owner and create a bond between them. The quilt may be a symbol of friendship, caring, or important moments in the individual maker's or owner's life and/or important events or ideas. Sometimes quilts are made by a group of individuals, and there are additional benefits from the bond formed among the makers. Quilts have helped individuals recover from the loss of loved ones, make a statement about an issue that is important to that individual, and so on. Quilt communities or groups add to individuals' lives via education, friendship, and emotional and social support. Fund raising by quilters has helped families faced with an emergency. Individually or group produced quilts have provided psychological and physical comfort.

The making of products provides individuals with a sense of self worth and adds to their quality of life. The sharing of these products with others creates a link between the maker and new owner. When the individual also interacts with others interested in the same production process a support system may develop, providing additional benefits for the individual.

## *Endnote*

1. A thesis statement generally has a key word or idea. It contains the central idea of the essay answer or in a paper, the central idea of the paper. One should be aware that there are some occasions in writing a paper when a thesis statement is not appropriate (Hacker & Sommers, 2011, p. 16). See *A Writer's Reference* by Hacker and Sommers (2011).

CHAPTER TWO

# Commonly Used Terms/Assignments and Words that are Easily Confused

Misunderstanding may arise when poor communication occurs between students and instructors. There are some commonly used assignment and exam terms that students may interpret differently than the instructor. This section is designed to help you know what an instructor expects when these terms are utilized in a syllabus, an assignment, or on a test.

Among the most common assignment or exam terms are "list," "describe," "discuss," "analyze," and "synthesize." Another term that is used in higher education is critical thinking. Each of these terms is asking for a different level of learning. To list is the simplest, least complex task, whereas to analyze, synthesize, and think critically are much more complex learning tasks.

## Commonly Used Terms/Assignments

### List

When asked to list something the student is expected give a series of words or phrases related to the specific subject/topic. In some cases a list is a series of categories.

*Examples:*

*List the different silhouette styles that have occurred over time in western women's garments.*

*Answer:* tubular, hourglass, backfullness

*List three orders of Greek architecture.*

*Answer:* Doric, Iconic, and Corinthian

### Describe

If you are asked to describe something, what is expected is an answer that clearly depicts or portrays what that item is; it should present a clear picture to the reader. Unless you are also asked to explain, a "describe" question only requires a description.

*Example:*

*Describe a Roman throne chair.*

*Answer:* barrel-shaped chair designed with animal legs having animal feet, other leg styles with animal feet, rectangular legs with decorative carvings, or turned legs. A tub chair version of the Roman throne had the back and sides designed in one unit with a circular shape and usually a solid base instead of legs.

## Compare/Contrast

If you are asked to *compare* two or more items, usually what is desired is to discuss their similarities as well as contrasting them by discussing their differences. If, however, you are asked to *contrast* two or more items you are being asked to *only* discuss the differences.

There are several ways to present a comparison. You may discuss one subject first and then discuss the second subject. Or, you can design your discussion in such a way that you compare and contrast the two subjects together, one aspect at a time.

> *Example:*
>
> *Compare the Greek Doric order with the Roman Doric order.*
>
> *Answer Number 1* (discussing first the Greek Doric, followed by the Roman Doric):
>
> The Greek Doric order consists of a massive, sharply fluted column shaft without a base; it rests directly on the platform. The column is slightly wider in the middle than at the base and narrows towards the top of the shaft. The Doric capital has no sculptural decoration and is composed of two parts: the echinus (a cushion-shaped molding) and the upper part, the abacus (a plain square block). The three parts of the entablature (the horizontal, upper part of the order) are generally fairly plain. The architrave is usually plain but is sometimes decorated with small triangular carvings in intermittent rows. The frieze is typically composed of triglyphs (rectangular shapes with vertical flutings) alternating with metopes (squares left plain or carved). At the top the cornice, which projects outward, is composed of several plain moldings with a decorated bottom surface.
>
> The Roman Doric order consists of a slender fluted column resting on a base; the bottom of the shaft has several plain moldings. The capital, though lacking much sculptural detail, has several moldings. The three parts of the entablature are generally fairly plain; the architrave is usually without detail, the frieze is typically composed of triglyphs alternating with metopes, and the cornice is composed of several plain moldings.
>
> *Answer Number 2* (comparing and contrasting the Greek and Roman Doric orders together, point by point):
>
> Both the Greek Doric column and the Roman Doric column have fluted shafts. However, there the similarity stops. The Greek Doric column rests directly on the platform; the Roman Doric column rests on a base, and the base of the column has several moldings. The shaft of the Greek Doric column is massive and heavy in appearance. It is slightly wider in the middle than at the base and then narrows toward the top. The Romans designed their Doric columns to be slender in appearance. The capital of the Greek Doric column is composed of two elements, the echinus (a cushion-shaped molding) and the abacus on top (a plain square block). The capital of the Roman Doric column, though still plain, has a number of plain moldings. Thus, in comparison to the Greek Doric capital, the Roman Doric capital is more complex. The entablature (the horizontal, upper part of the order) of both the Greek and Roman Doric orders is composed of an architrave, frieze, and cornice. Often one can see little difference between the Greek and Roman Doric entablatures.

## Discuss

To discuss means to present a detailed examination or consideration of an idea or concept. You may want to begin by describing the appropriate components, but *a discussion goes beyond a description*. Generally a well-written discussion demonstrates that the writer is knowledgeable on the subject.

> *Example:*
>
> *Discuss the influences on menswear in the 19th century and their consequences.*

*Answer:* Men of the upper class, prior to the 18th century, wore a variety of colors and patterns in their dress. However, menswear of the 19th century is very sober in appearance. Some scholars see the beginning of this trend starting in the latter half of 18th century England with the middle class reacting to the excesses of the upper class and the upper class responding to this style shift. Another influence that is sometimes given is that of the nonconformist religious groups such as the Quakers (Breward, 1995, p.134). Nineteenth century influences on men's dress include new technological inventions and social ideas about what were appropriate masculine styles (Breward, 1995, p. 147). Though ready-made apparel had been available prior to the 19th century, it became much more available and prevalent in the 19th century. In England one of the influences on this change was the development of the railroad as well as the development and success of department stores and the invention of the sewing machine (Chenoune, 1993, p. 67). Although factory-produced textiles began appearing in the late 18th century, it took until the 20th century before the majority of menswear was factory-produced. More and more garments were produced utilizing an assembly line process, and there was a change in the variety of design and individual fitting of men's garments. Pattern making and the accompanying skills of grading, cutting, and pressing were nonexistent or in their infancy during this period. This was reflected in the appearance of menswear. Much of the menswear produced during these early stages of factory production was of poor quality. Additionally, with the coming of factory production, the variety of styles slowly began to diminish as factory owners recognized cost savings by limiting variety. Menswear became more somber in color partly due to the dirt and soot from factories and coal-powered steam engines and also due to the change in attitudes brought about by changing lifestyles and class influence as a result of the Industrial Revolution. By the end of the century, business suits had arrived and were relatively dull, drab, and practical looking—quite a contrast to the pastel silk brocade outfits of the 18th century.

Note how this answer goes beyond just listing influences or pure description of menswear and actually discusses how the influences contributed to changes in menswear.

## Analyze

When one analyzes something, it is examined in detail, and the nature and relationship of the individual parts or components are studied with regard to how they contribute to the whole. In writing up an analysis, you should be sure to describe the item or idea in detail, but also discuss how the individual parts, ideas, and components contribute to the whole. A synonym of analysis is dissection.

*Example:*

*Analyze how the Smith business operates.*

*The analysis process:* To analyze how the Smith business operates, it would first be necessary to determine all of the individual components of the business. One might start by determining how many employees there are and their individual roles and responsibilities. If the Smith business is large, one might identify all the different departments and what role each department plays. One would need to determine who the decision makers are and who acts upon decisions (i.e., those who follow the orders of the decision makers). It would also be necessary to determine how well orders were carried out. Sometimes it is useful to draw models (diagrams) of the different components and to utilize lines with directional arrows to demonstrate how the different parts/individuals interact.

If you are asked in a test question or a paper for an analysis, think about the subject of the analysis and discuss its components and how each component contributes to the whole. For instance: if asked to analyze the influences affecting a particular design period, you would describe each influence and discuss how each individual influence shaped the styles of that period. You would include in this discussion what was the particular contribution of each influence.

## Apply

In the sciences one often hears the terms "pure science" and "applied science." Application of an idea is defined as "the use to which something can or should be put" (DK Publishing, 1998, p. 47). If you can apply an idea or discuss the application of an idea, you are moving from the abstract theoretical to the practical.

> *Example:*
>
> *Discuss the fashion process in a historical context. Select a fashion theory and demonstrate the basic premise of the theory by applying it to a specific period in time.*
>
> *Answer:* The fashion theory known as the trickle down theory best fits the fashion process of the Late Middle Ages. The basic premise of this theory is that fashionable styles originate among the members of the upper class and are copied by the classes below, trickling down to the lower classes. It is also called the upper-class leadership theory (Sproles & Burns, 1994, p. 110). "The theory also implies that the upper classes adopt new fashion as symbols of exclusiveness and differentiation from the social inferiors" (Sproles & Burns, p. 110). Among scholars there is general agreement that the social phenomena or fashion process began in the Late Middle Ages. When societal institutions began to change in the Late Middle Ages, a market economy and capitalism began to develop, the influence of the church became less strong, and Western European world views began to change. Fashion developed, and the fashion process became a strong influence on apparel and other product styles. Initially it was royalty and nobility who clothed themselves in the newest apparel styles, including the newest textiles, and furnished their homes in the latest styles. With the spread of wealth to the upper middle class, "members of the bourgeoisie began to use clothing not only to separate themselves from other social classes and assert their social position, but also to express their individual personality" (Lehnert, 1998, p. 11). The nobility, wishing to appear different from the bourgeoisie, would then adopt new fashion styles. An example of fashionable styles from the Late Middle Ages is the poulaine or crackow (the shoe with the extremely pointed toe worn to show one's class superiority). By the "end of the 15th century, style changes were occurring at least every several decades instead of taking a hundred or more years" (Tortora & Eubank, 2010, p. 8). The fashionable styles continued to begin among members of the upper class and trickled down for several hundred years.

## Synthesize

Synthesis is the combining of parts or elements to form a whole. Often synthesis is utilized in problem solving. When you write a paper you begin by collecting information. That information is not necessarily arranged in the order in which you can or wish to utilize it. In the process of writing the paper you synthesize the various ideas and facts which you have collected and add your own ideas on the subject. The resultant paper is a synthesis of other individuals' ideas and facts (with citations showing the source of these ideas and facts) with your own. A synthesis can contain one or more sections of analysis; however, the entire synthesis combines and brings together the section(s) of analysis.

> *Example:* Assume that you had been hired as a consultant to help a business run more efficiently. You would probably begin by analyzing the business's operations as discussed under "Analyze." To solve the problem of efficiency, you would take all of your knowledge and experience (as well as possibly doing some research on efficiency in similar businesses) and combine your findings with your knowledge to develop a solution. The solution would be the synthesis or combining together of your results (your analysis of the company and your research on efficiency) with your suggestions to the business owner(s) for how to improve their business.

If a test question or paper guidelines include the word "synthesis" then you will want to think about the individual components that you are being asked to synthesize, how they can relate to each other, and how they can contribute to the end product/answer you are being asked to develop.

### Critical thinking

When you write, whether an essay exam or an assigned paper, your instructors hope you will show evidence of understanding what others have said about the topic at hand. Beyond that they hope you show evidence of *critical thinking*. Writing that demonstrates critical thinking shows the use of "a sophisticated skill set rather than . . . rote learning" (Carmichael & Farrell, 2012, "The nature of critical thinking," para. 1). The critical thinking skill set includes the following processes: analyzing, reflecting, relating, questioning, making judgments, and synthesizing information. Critical thinking goes beyond personal opinion or merely "quoting scholarly authors" (Jones, 2013, para. 2). Critical thinking is about the how and why of a subject or idea not the what, when, and where. Evidence of critical thinking includes using and understanding complex ideas, using information and ideas, or evidence from reliable sources that help support your work, providing "justifications and . . . explanations" in your writing (Jones, para. 3). In fact, an important part of writing that shows evidence of critical thinking is the use of in text citations which document the source of your information. Other aspects of critical thinking are comparing and contrasting views and ideas, providing problem-solving responses (Jones, para. 5, bullets), "assessment, examination, reflective reasoning of existing information, ideas, beliefs, and speculations" (Jones, 2013, "Helping Students Think Critically," para. 2).

## Words that are Easily Confused

There are a number of words that are often confused with each other. Sometimes a spelling or punctuation error turns the word we thought we wrote into its confusing "twin." Other times the error is because we cannot remember which word it is we want to use, or we are unaware of the difference. This is often a case where the "spell check" feature on our word processing software is of no use because the word we have written is not misspelled. The following list of examples is by no means exhaustive but includes the most common errors made by students. If you are unsure, use a dictionary or ask your instructor.

### Accept, except

*Accept* is a verb (generally communicates action) that means "to receive." *Except* generally is used as a preposition (a word that is put before a noun or pronoun to make a phrase that modifies another word in the sentence) and means "excluding."

Examples: The student *accepted* the grade the instructor wrote on her project; she knew she had earned it.

The student had included all of the course illustrations in her portfolio *except* the one she completed during the first week of the course.

## Affect, effect

*Affect* is usually a verb; it means "to influence." *Affect* is sometimes used as a noun; when *affect* is used as a noun, it is an emotion or feeling attached to an object or idea or a disposition or tendency. *Effect* is generally a noun (the name of an idea, person, place, or thing) and means "result." *Effect* is sometimes used as a verb; when *effect* is used as a verb it means "to bring about."

*Examples:* Taking the quiz the day before Thanksgiving appeared to have *affected* the students' scores.

Positive *affect* on the part of the teacher is pleasing to students.

The *effect* of the higher energy prices resulted in an increase in the use of energy efficient appliances by homeowners.

To *effect* a change in consumers' behavior sometimes is quite difficult.

## I, me

*I* is a pronoun (a word used instead of a noun) that functions as a subject, while *me* is a pronoun that functions as an object.

*Examples:* The student told the instructor, "*I* am going to earn an 'A' on my project."

The student told the instructor, "That is my project; it belongs to *me*."

## That, which, who

*That* is generally used to refer to things, but it can be used to refer to a group of people. *Which* should not be used to refer to persons; use *who*. Additionally, *that* is usually used for restrictive adjective clauses (an adjective clause modifies a noun or a pronoun) and *which* is used for nonrestrictive adjective clauses. A nonrestrictive adjective clause has information that is not essential to the meaning of the sentence and is usually set off with commas. A restrictive adjective clause is essential to the meaning of the sentence; if it is removed the meaning will change, and thus commas are not used.

*Examples:* Proponents of the trickle-down theory state *that* fashions are adopted first by the members of the upper class and then each descending class adopts them as they trickle-down to the lowest class.

Those *who* chose to spend more money can buy designer jeans.

The house, *which* was a neo-Gothic style, was painted in shades of blue.

Be sure to take the chair *that* has the saber legs and lyre back with you.

## There, their, they're

*There* is an adverb (used to modify a verb, adjective, or another adverb) related to the idea of place and can be replaced with *here*. There is also an expletive (an expletive is used to fill in a vacancy in a sentence without changing the meaning). *Their* is a possessive pronoun and can be replaced with our, and *they're* is a contraction of they are.

*Examples:* I went to Paris on a study tour last summer; it is fantastic there. (In this sentence *there* is used as an adverb.)

*There* is a Doric column. (In this sentence *there* is used as an expletive.)

*Their* design won the competition.

*They're* going on the tour to Italy.

## To, too, two

*To* is a preposition while *too* is an adverb. *Two* is a number.

*Examples:* He is going *to* the library.

There are *too* many chairs in this room.

There are *two* correct answers for question 11.

## Your, you're

*Your* is a possessive pronoun; *you're* is a contraction of *you are*.

*Examples:* May I borrow *your* notes?

I understand that *you're* about to be nominated for president of your club.

# CHAPTER THREE

# Some Rules of Writing and the American Psychological Association (APA) Style

Consistency in our communication styles helps us understand each other; this is true of both verbal and written communication. In the case of verbal communication, you can ask for clarification if you do not understand what is being said. However, in written communication, the writer typically is not present to help clarify what was meant. Thus it is very important in writing that the use of words and the arrangement of words, sentences, and paragraphs make sense to the reader. Over time, this has prompted the development of rules for spelling, grammar, paragraph structure, and so forth. The careful writer not only learns the rules of writing and knows what style guide needs to be followed but also goes back to check for errors and mistakes when a particular writing project is finished.

In this section of the DHE style guide, the usual format for a formal paper is discussed along with lessening bias in communicating, using numbers, and the use of headings. This is followed by a discussion of how to structure reference citations within the text or body of the paper as well as in the reference section according to the style used by the American Psychological Association (APA). The APA style is the style most frequently used by the Design and Human Environment faculty's professional organizations.

## Format of the Paper

Typically a paper has three parts: the front pieces, the text, and the references. The front piece may be only a title page or may also include a preface, table of contents, list of tables, and list of illustrations. The text usually has an introduction, the main body of the paper, and a summary and/or conclusion. The paper is followed by a reference section and sometimes an appendix.

### Text introduction

An introduction usually contains the purpose of the paper and states the main points that will be discussed. Ideally the purpose will also contain statements that will interest the reader and encourage continued reading of the paper.

### The main body

The main part of your paper supports the main point(s) you established in the introduction. Before beginning this part of your paper you may want to develop an outline by writing the main idea and then listing the supporting ideas. Generally, in order to develop your main idea and find support for your ideas (the text) you will need to search for reliable sources of information (see Chapter 4 for ideas on how to determine the reliability of sources). After developing your list of supporting ideas you may find that you wish to rearrange the order. When you have ordered your ideas in a logical manner you can begin writing. Plan on writing at least one paragraph for each supporting idea. If the main body of the paper warrants it, headings may be used to subdivide the paper into sections; typically the sections are related to your individual supporting ideas (see below for a discussion of headings and the APA heading style).

### Summary/conclusion

You will end your paper with a summary and/or a conclusion. There is a difference between a summary and a conclusion. A summary "summarizes" (i.e., presents the information from the body of the paper in an abbreviated form). A conclusion may include a summary, but, more importantly, a conclusion contains a discussion in which you express your ideas and thoughts on the topic including a discussion of the relevance of your topic to your field of study (e.g., design, merchandising, and so forth). A conclusion provides evidence of your critical thinking abilities and is often required by instructors. Be sure to ask if your instructor wishes you to have a summary or a conclusion for the ending of your paper.

In the American Psychological Association (APA) style the reference section includes a list of references for all of the works that you have cited within the body of your paper but does *not* include any sources that were not cited in the text. There is a specific APA reference style that is discussed later in this chapter. In addition, some writers use an appendix. The appendix (or appendices) is placed at the end of the paper and contains supplementary information that is related to the topic of the paper but would be distracting if included in the body of the paper.

## Lessening Bias in Communication

Most organizations and institutions are committed to treating individuals and groups fairly. This commitment is shared by many organizations including the American Psychological Association. This organization has developed style guidelines to help lessen bias in language (*Publication Manual*, 2010, pp. 70–77).

In your writing it is important to "avoid perpetuating demeaning attitudes and biased assumptions about people in . . . writing. Constructions that might imply bias against persons on the basis of gender, sexual orientation, racial or ethnic group, disability, or age are unacceptable" (*Publication Manual*, 2010, pp. 70–71).

It is important to check your work for bias before turning it in; habitual ways of writing may include unintended bias. Generally, "differences [among individuals or groups] should be mentioned only when relevant" (*Publication Manual*, 2010, p. 71).

The writers of the APA *Publication Manual* provide guidelines to be considered. Sometimes following the guidelines may lead to clumsy writing; you will have to use your judgment. The desired end result is accurate, unbiased communication (*Publication Manual*, 2010, p. 71). See "Reducing Bias in Language" and "Reducing Bias by Topic" in Chapter 3 of the *Publication Manual* (2010), "Writing Clearly and Concisely: Reducing Bias by Topic: Sexual Orientation" on the APA Style Web site (www.apastyle.org/style), and "Using Nonsexist Language" on the OSU Writing Center Web site (http://cwl.oregonstate.edu/sites/default/files/writing_tips_handouts/h-nsex.html) for examples. The APA guidelines are briefly discussed below.

### "Guideline 1: Describe at the appropriate level of specificity" (*Publication Manual,* 2010, p. 71)

Use words that are "accurate, clear, and free from bias" (*Publication Manual*, p. 71). If you are unsure, be more specific as opposed to less specific. For instance, use a specific age range instead of being more general ("ages 70 to 85" instead of "over 70" or use Korean Americans and Japanese Americans instead of Asian Americans).

*Gender* is cultural and is the term to use when referring to women and men as social groups. Sex is biological; use it when the biological distinction is predominant. . . . differences should be mentioned only when relevant. Marital status, sexual orientation, racial and ethnic identity, or the fact that a person has a disability should not be mentioned gratuitously. (*Publication Manual*, 2010, p. 71)

### "Guideline 2: Be sensitive to labels" (*Publication Manual*, 2010, pp. 72–73).

Use the term the individuals you are writing about prefer; try to find out what is appropriate. "Call people what they prefer to be called" (p. 72). Be willing to ask individuals what designation they want. In general, avoid labeling individuals.

Avoid categorizing groups as objects (e.g., *the young* or *the married*). You can use adjectives such as *young people*, *young individuals*, or *married individuals*. Also, sometimes the order in which groups or individuals are presented may imply a standard or rank order so "avoid a consistent pattern of presenting information about socially dominant groups first" (*Publication Manual*, 2010, p. 73).

### "Guideline 3: Acknowledge participation" (*Publication Manual*, 2010, p. 73)

When writing about a study, acknowledge the participants. Generally, instead of using *subjects* and *sample* use the following terms: *participants, individuals, college students, children,* or *respondents*. However, "*subjects* and *sample* are customary when discussing certain established statistical terms" (p. 73). For further discussion of lessening bias in communication, refer to pages 70 to 77 (Sections 3.11 to 3.17) in the 6th edition of the *Publication Manual of the American Psychological Association* (2010).

## Using Numbers

"The general rule governing APA style on the use of numbers is to use numerals to express numbers 10 and above and words to express numbers below 10" (*Publication Manual*, 2010, p. 111).

### "Numbers expressed in numerals" (*Publication Manual*, 2010, pp. 111–112)

Numerals are used to express:

- any number 10 and above; for exceptions see below. *Example:* There were 10 bedrooms in the house.
- "numbers. . . in a graphical display within a paper" (*Publication Manual*, 2010, p. 111). Thus in a chart, graph, or other figure use numerals.
- "numbers that immediately precede a unit of measurement" (p. 111). *Example:* The garment measured 23 inches in the waist.
- "numbers that represent statistical or mathematical functions, fractional or decimal quantities, percentages, ratios, and percentiles and quartiles" (p. 111). *Examples:* In fact 10% of the group; the Golden Mean ratio is 1:1.618.
- "numbers that represent time, dates, ages, scores and points on a scale, exact sums of money, and numerals as numerals" (p. 112). *Example:* Brunelleschi designed the dome of the Florence Cathedral in 1418.
- any number that indicates a specific position in a series or book such as a table or figure or any number that is "in a list of four or more numbers" (p. 112). *Example:* Figure 5, numbers 2, 5, 7, and 10.

### "Numbers expressed in words" (*Publication Manual,* 2010, p. 112)

Words are used to express:

- Numbers that are at the beginning of a title or a sentence. *Example*: Twenty-two percent of the people in Oregon are under 18 years of age ("State & County," 2013).
- Common fractions. *Example:* Just over one half of the Oregon population is female ("State & County," 2013).

### "Combining numerals and words to express numbers" (*Publication Manual,* 2010, pp. 112–113)

A combination of words and numerals is used with back-to-back modifiers; this "increases the clarity and readability of the construction" (p. 113). *Example:* The blouse featured 2 two-inch tucks.

For further discussion of expressing numbers, refer to pages 111 to 114 (Sections 4.31 to 4.38) in the 6th edition of the *Publication Manual of the American Psychological Association.*

## Abbreviations

It is a good idea to avoid using abbreviations. Appropriate use of abbreviations would include standard titles such as *Mr., Ms.,* and *Dr.* Also appropriate would be abbreviations for well known organizations, corporations, states, and the United States:

```
FBI

IBM

YMCA

OR

WA

USA (or U.S.A.)
```

Another situation in which use of abbreviations is appropriate is if there are standard abbreviations that are understood by all within your area of study. Also, consider your audience when you write. If you are writing to the general public do not use abbreviations that are specific to your profession.

If too many abbreviations are used in one sentence or paragraph, it may cause confusion. Generally it is best to avoid abbreviations that are not conventional. Do not use abbreviations if by doing so you will confuse your reader.

It is best not to use A.M. or P.M. when not accompanied by a specific time. For example, if you wish to discuss something that happened in the evening but not at a specific time, use the word evening.

Some writers make use of Latin abbreviations. These should be used sparingly and should be used "only in parenthetical material [i.e., within parentheses]; in non-parenthetical material, use the English translation of the Latin terms; in both cases, include the correct punctuation that accompanies the term" (*Publication Manual*, 2010, p. 108):

| | |
|---|---|
| e.g., | for example |
| etc. | and so forth |
| i.e., | that is |
| viz., | namely |
| vs. | versus, against |

*Examples:* There are many different types of chairs; for example, barrel chairs, rocking chairs, spindle-back chairs, and so forth.

There are many different types of chairs (e.g., barrel chairs, rocking chairs, spindle-back chairs, etc.).

For further discussion of abbreviations refer to pages 106 to 111 (Sections 4.22 to 4.30) in the 6th edition of the *Publication Manual of the American Psychological Association.*

## Headings and Levels of Headings

If a paper or a section of a paper is particularly long, it is often appropriate to use headings to help the reader understand the organization of the section or the paper. Headings can help indicate the importance of each topic. For each topic that is of the same level of importance, you would use the same type or level of heading. Sometimes it is useful to use subheadings. However, you should "avoid having only one subsection heading and subsection within a section, just as you would in an outline" (*Publication Manual*, 2010, p. 62). You should have two or more subsection headings or none at all. Typically the introduction does not have a heading.

If you use an outline in writing your paper, you may find your outline useful in determining the wording of your headings. Or, if you need to review your paper for organization, the development of headings may help you with your organization.

In APA style it is possible to have five levels of headings. The five types of headings are presented below in order of importance and order of use:

**Centered, Boldface, Uppercase and Lowercase Heading [Level 1]**

**Flush Left, Boldface, Uppercase and Lowercase Heading [Level 2]**

**Indented, bold face, lowercase paragraph heading ending with a period. [Level 3]**

***Indented, boldface, italicized, lowercase paragraph heading ending with a period.* [Level 4]**

*Indented, italicized, lowercase paragraph heading ending with a period.* [Level 5] (*Publication Manual*, 2010, p. 63).

Note: the last three headings (indented ending with a period) are used as the starting point of a paragraph. The first sentence of the paragraph begins immediately after the heading on the same line. Levels one and two headings are placed above the beginning of the first paragraph of new sections. See the examples below.

*Example 1:*

**Garment Terms**

**Types of Garments**

**Jackets.** The text (discussing jackets in general) follows this level of heading and begins immediately after the period at the end of the heading.

***Dress jackets.*** The text (discussing dress jackets) follows this level of heading and begins immediately after the period at the end of the heading.

***Sport jackets.*** The text (discussing sport jackets in general) follows this level of heading and begins immediately after the period at the end of the heading.

*Baseball jackets.* The text (discussing baseball jackets) follows this level of heading and begins immediately after the period at the end of the heading.

*Snowboarding jackets.* The text (discussing snowboarding jackets) follows this level of heading and begins immediately after the period at the end of the heading.

**Dresses.** Since "jackets" and "dresses" are not the only types of garments more headings at this level would follow. Depending upon the specific type of garment most likely there would be some level 4 and level 5 headings used as well.

**Types of Collars**

**Notched collar.** As discussed above the text follows immediately after this heading.

**Shawl collar.** As discussed above the text follows immediately after this heading.

Other Level 2 headings would follow identifying other garment part types. Most of these would have at least some level 3 headings and some might have level 4 and/or level 5 headings as well.

**Conclusion**

Note how each descending heading becomes more specific. The most general components of your paper, if you utilized all five heading levels, would be found under the centered uppercase heading, and the most specific parts of your paper would be found under the indented, italicized, lowercase paragraph heading which ends with a period.

*Example 2:* If you utilize only one level of heading, then a boldface centered uppercase and lowercase heading is used.

**Medieval Furniture**

**Renaissance Furniture**

**Baroque Furniture**

*Example 3:* This example breaks furniture down into period furniture and contemporary furniture. There are three "types" of period furniture discussed (Renaissance, French Baroque, and English Restoration) and two types of contemporary furniture.

**Period Furniture**

**Renaissance**

**French Baroque**

**English Restoration**

**Contemporary Furniture**

**Pre World War II**

**Post World War II**

*Example 4:* As mentioned, one does not have to have the same number of headings under each main (or first level) heading. However, it is always necessary to have at least two headings of the same level in the same section of the paper. The "xx's" in the example below represent text.

**Literature Review**

**Xxx Xxxxx  Xxxxxx**

Xxxx xxxxx xxxxx xx x xxxxxxxxxx xxxx xxxxxx xxxx. Xxxx xxx xx xxxxxxxx xx x xxxxxx xx xxxxxxxxx. Xxx xxxx x xxxxxxxxxx xx. Xxx xxxx x xxxxxxxxxx xx. Xxx xxxxxx xxxxx xxx xxx xxxx. Xxxx xxxxx xxxxx xx x xxxxxxxxxx xxxx xxxxxx xxxx. Xxxx xxx xx xxxxxxxx xx x xxxxxx xx xxxxxxxxx. Xxx xxxx x xxxxxxxxxx xx. Xxxx xxxxx xxxxx xx x xxxxxxxxxx xxxx xxxxxx xxxx.

**Xxx Xxxxxxxxxx**

Xxx xxxxx xx xxxxxxx xxxx xxxxxxx. Xxx xxxx x xxxxxxxxxx xx. Xxxx xxxxx xxxxx xx x xxxxxxxxxx xxxx xxxxxx xxxx. Xxxx xxx xx xxxxxxxx xx x xxxxxx xx xxxxxxxxx. Xxx xxxx x xxxxxxxxxx xx. Xxxx xxxxx xxxxx xx x xxxxxxxxxx xxxx xxxxxx xxxx. Xxx xxxx x xxxxxxxxxx xx. Xxx xxxxxx xxxxx xxx xxx xxxx. Xxx xxxx xx xx xxx.

**Research Design**

Xxx xxxx x xxxxxxxxxx xx. Xxxx xxxxx xxxxx xx x xxxxxxxxxx xxxx xxxxxx xxxx. Xxxx xxx xx xxxxxxxx xx x xxxxxx xx xxxxxxxxx. Xxx xxxx x xxxxxxxxxx xx. Xxxx xxxxx xxxxx xx x xxxxxxxxxx xxxx xxxxxx xxxx. Xxx xxxx x xxxxxxxxxx xx. Xxx xxxxxx xxxxx xxx xxx xxxx. Xxxx xxxxx xxxxx xx x xxxxxxxxxx xxxx xxxxxx xxxx. Xxxx xxx xx xxxxxxxx xx x xxxxxx xx xxxxxxxxx. Xxx xxxx x xxxxxxxxxx xx. Xxxx xxxxx xxxxx xx x xxxxxxxxxx xxxx xxxxxx xxxx. Xxxxx xxxxxx xx x xxxx xxxx xxxxxx xx xx xxxxxx xxxxx.

**Experimental Research**

Xxx xxxx x xxxxxxxxxx xx. Xxxx xxxxx xxxxx xx x xxxxxxxxxx xxxx xxxxxx xxxx. Xxxx xxx xx xxxxxxxx xx x xxxxxx xx xxxxxxxxx. Xxx xxxx x xxxxxxxxxx xx. Xxxx xxxxx xxxxx xx x xxxxxxxxxx xxxx xxxxxx xxxx.

**Method**

xxxxxxx xxxx xx xxxxxxxxxx xxx xxxxxx xxxxxx. xxx xxxxx xx xxxxxxxxxxx. Xxxx xxxxx xxxxx xx x xxxxxxxxxx xxxx xxxxxx xxxx.

**Instrument development.** Xxx xxxx x xxxxxxxxxx xx. Xxxx xxxxx xxxxx xx x xxxxxxxxxx xxxx xxxxxx xxxx. Xxxx xxx xx xxxxxxxx xx x xxxxxx xx xxxxxxxxx. Xxx xxxx x xxxxxxxxxx xx. Xxxx xxxxx xxxxx xx x xxxxxxxxxx xxxx xxxxxx xxxx.

**Sample.** Xxx xxxx x xxxxxxxxxx xx. Xxx xxxxxx xxxxx xxx xxx xxxx. Xxxx xxxxx xxxxx xx x xxxxxxxxxx xxxx xxxxxx xxxx. Xxxx xxx xx xxxxxxxx xx x xxxxxx xx xxxxxxxxx. Xxx xxxx x xxxxxxxxxx xx. Xxxx xxxxx xxxxx xx x xxxxxxxxxx xxxx xxxxxx xxxx. Xxxxx xxxxxx xx x xxxx xxxx xxxxxx xx xx xxxxxx xxxxx.

**Data collection.** Xxx xxxx x xxxxxxxxxx xx. Xxxx xxxxx xxxxx xx x xxxxxxxxxx xxxx xxxxxx xxxx. Xxxx xxx xx xxxxxxxx xx x xxxxxx xx xxxxxxxxx. Xxx xxxx x xxxxxxxxxx xx. Xxxx xxxxx xxxxx xx x xxxxxxxxxx xxxx xxxxxx xxxx. Xxx xxxx x xxxxxxxxxx xx. Xxx xxxxxx xxxxx xxx xxx xxxx. Xxxx xxxxx xxxxx xx x xxxxxxxxxx xxxx xxxxxx xxxx. Xxxx xxx xx xxxxxxxx xx x xxxxxx xx xxxxxxxxx. Xxx xxxx x xxxxxxxxxx xx. Xxxx xxxxx xxxxx xx x xxxxxxxxxx xxxx xxxxxx xxxx. Xxxxx xxxxxx xx x xxxx xxxx xxxxxx xx xx xxxxxx xxxxx.

**Data analysis.** Xxx xxxx x xxxxxxxxxx xx. Xxx xxxxxx xxxxx xxx xxx xxxx. Xxxx xxxxx xxxxx xx x xxxxxxxxxx xxxx xxxxxx xxxx. Xxxx xxx xx xxxxxxxx xx x xxxxxx xx xxxxxxxxx. Xxx xxxx x xxxxxxxxxx xx. Xxxx xxxxx xxxxx xx x xxxxxxxxxx xxxx xxxxxx xxxx. Xxxxx xxxxxx xx x xxxx xxxx xxxxxx xx xx xxxxxx xxxxx.

**Results**

**Conclusion**

## Using the Work of Others

In much of your written work you will make use of the thoughts, ideas, and findings of scholars. You will have assignments in which the expectation is that you will collect scholars' views and research results and conclusions to help you develop conclusions of your own (this is part of thinking critically).

In writing up your work, it is important that you acknowledge the work of others. Whether you are completing a library research project, a literature review, or some other written work, it is important that you learn how to take notes from written materials and record the complete bibliographic information for each source you have used. A very basic rule is: Do not rely on your memory and take care and time in writing your notes and the bibliographic information.

A very important part of using others' ideas is that it is not considered appropriate to change words in a quotation. When possible keep copies of your sources (e.g., photocopy or scan relevant pages and title pages with bibliographic information, photocopy or scan journal articles, etc.). This is particularly important with items you find on Web sites. Remember that electronic items may not always be available, or the page may have been rewritten when you need to go back and confirm your information (Hacker & Sommers, 2011, p. 359). Before you end each library session or Web search make sure that you have full bibliographic information for each source, you have clearly marked exact quotes, and you have checked to be sure to avoid bad paraphrasing (Storey, 1999, p. 26).

Think about how you wish to take notes with regard to avoiding intentional plagiarism. What you do not want to do is have part of your notes use the author's words and the rest of your notes be poor paraphrasing of the author's words. This, most likely, will lead to plagiarism. Thus there are two methods of note-taking that tend to prevent unintentional plagiarism. With the first method, read the relevant section and then take notes without looking at what you have just read. By doing this you are more likely to use your own words and be truly paraphrasing the author's work. However, it is important that you double check and make sure you have not inadvertently poorly paraphrased (Hacker & Sommers, 2011, p. 361). In the second method, take all of your notes in direct quotes. Use quotation marks to identify the beginning and ending of each quotation and in parentheses use the correct APA text citation so that you clearly identify the source of the quotation. If you think that in using the first method you will inadvertently plagiarize, then use the second method.

## Reference Citations within the Paper—In-text Citations

In papers when you utilize the work of others, it is important to document and thus acknowledge their work and ideas; documenting needs to be done for paraphrasing and direct quotations. Documentation is accomplished by creating in-text citations. In-text citations tell readers which sources you have used, and equally important, credit is given to the person whose ideas and knowledge you have used (Hacker & Sommers, 2011, p. 448). In-text citations of the reference materials used to develop your paper recognize the scholars who "contributed to your work" (*Publication Manual*, 2010, p. 169). Additionally, if you have chosen appropriate and quality sources then using citations demonstrates credibility and allows readers to know where to seek more in-depth information on your paper topic.

### Plagiarism

Many students incorrectly believe that a citation is necessary only when a direct quote is used. This is incorrect; the purpose of citations is to acknowledge the work and ideas of others. Use a citation whether it is a direct quote or a paraphrase of the information.

The following are all regarded as plagiarism: (1) failing to cite quotations and borrowed ideas, (2) failing to enclose borrowed language in quotation marks (or to use indented blocked quotes for long quotations), and (3) failing to put summaries and paraphrases in your own words (Hacker & Sommers, 2011, p. 376).

As discussed, an in-text citation acknowledges that you have used the work of a specific individual or group of individuals. Therefore the expectation is that you will cite ALL sources of the information you have collected and used in your writing unless the information is general knowledge. "Cite the work of those individuals whose ideas, theories, or research have directly influenced your work" (*Publication Manual*, 2010, p. 169). This influence can include any or all of the following: "background information, support or dispute of your thesis, or . . . critical definitions and data" (*Publication Manual*, 2010, p. 169). Additionally, if you use any factual information that is not well known provide a citation.

Visuals are also information; they represent ideas, and they are the work of individuals. When you use or discuss a visual (illustration, photograph, etc.) credit the creator, whether an individual, company, or organization. If you do not give credit when you have used others' ideas and work then you have plagiarized the material. This is a serious offense.

Plagiarism occurs when an individual represents others' work as his or her own; plagiarism can be intentional or unintentional. Plagiarism includes using the exact words from a written source (i.e., a quotation), failing to put this direct copying of phrases, sentences, and paragraphs in quotation marks, and failing to use a text citation acknowledging the source of the words. Plagiarism also occurs when someone else's ideas are used without a text citation *even if* the writer does not directly quote from the original source or the idea has not yet been published. Plagiarism may be defined as theft—stealing another person's work and creativity without acknowledgement. What is really at issue is a matter of ethics, academic integrity, and honesty. The discovery of plagiarism by an instructor in a student's work will mean at the very least embarrassment and a poor grade. However, it may also result in expulsion from the university. For a faculty member, it might result in loss of funding or job and the scorn of colleagues.

> Another important point is that as you progress in your education the standards become higher. As a College student you are expected to have your own ideas. To read information and explain it in your words. If you complete an assignment by copying material, you are not showing that you understand something. Only that you can repeat what the textbook says. This does not show that you understand. (Van Bramer, 1995, Introduction)

Plagiarism may occur accidently due to ignorance, laziness, or sloppy technique; it may also be done intentionally. Sometimes plagiarism occurs because the writer does not know the correct method of citation. Other times plagiarism occurs because the writer is unsure what the term plagiarism means.

To avoid plagiarizing, **cite your source**

1. when you use quotation marks and a direct quote,
2. when you rewrite or paraphrase several authors' words in the same paragraph,
3. if you refer to an author's idea(s), or
4. whenever you use an author's name ("Plagiarism," 2010–2012, "How Can I tell Whether I've Plagiarized?").

Your best course of action is to be conservative in your writing relative to plagiarism. It is rare that a student's work is downgraded for too many citations. If you are "in doubt, give a citation" ("Plagiarism," 2010–2012, "How Can I tell Whether I've Plagiarized?"). If you are unclear about what plagiarism is, discuss this issue with your instructor.

## Paraphrasing

Students sometimes misunderstand what is meant by paraphrasing.

> Paraphrasing means taking another person's ideas and putting those ideas in your own words. Paraphrasing does NOT mean changing a word or two in someone else's sentence, changing the sentence structure while maintaining the original words, or changing a few words to synonyms. If you are tempted to rearrange a sentence in any of these ways, you are writing too close to the original. That's plagiarizing, not paraphrasing. ("Plagiarism," 2010–2012, "What About Paraphrasing?")

Paraphrasing another individual's ideas is an accepted practice. As discussed under taking notes, the best way to paraphrase is for you to work with the book or article closed or not directly in front of you. Then you will be writing with your knowledge of the author's ideas but not constantly referring to the sentences and thus possibly plagiarizing. Do remember to check after you have finished making your notes to ensure you have not unintentionally plagiarized. Remember that you should use in-text citations for BOTH direct quotes and paraphrasing.

## In-text citations

There are different styles of citing sources. The "in-text" citation style, used by the American Psychological Association (APA), is used to provide information about the source within the written text, usually within parentheses. The APA style lists the author's last name and the date of the publication/source or the copyright date, known as the author-date method of citation, within parentheses, usually at the end of a sentence. The page number is always included in the text citation when citing a quotation or specific facts. In the APA style no endnotes or footnotes are used for text citations. See the variety of examples below of the APA in-text citation style within the text of a paper. If you do not see an example that fits your source, check with your instructor about how to cite your source.

***If a quote from a printed source is used***, place quotation marks around the quote and always include the page number from which the quote was taken in the in-text citation.

*Example:*

"Fit is how a garment conforms to or differs from the body" (Glock & Kunz, 2000, p. 111). Fit is one of the characteristics of product differentiation with price classifications.

Notice how the quotation marks at the end of the quotation come before the in-text citation and the period to end the sentence is placed after the in-text citation.

***If a quote from a Web source is used***, place quotation marks around the quote and always include the page number or paragraph number from which the quote was taken in the in-text citation.

*Example in which there are no page numbers, no identified author, and no copyright date:*

"Because plagiarism is considered a serious academic offense at Strayer University and a misdeed in the world in general, a student found plagiarizing will face consequences for his or her actions" ("Consequences of," n.d., para. 2).

In this example the Web site had no author and no copyright date. Thus instead of providing an author's name the first several words of the title are used in quotation marks. When there is no date this is abbreviated with "n.d." Do be aware that often there is a date but you may have to search for it. Notice the paragraph number in which the quote appeared is provided.

*Example in which there are no page numbers, no identified author, and article headings:*

"If the work does not have an author, cite the source by its title . . . use the first word or two in the parentheses" ("In-Text," 1995-2013, para. 1).

In this citation example it may look the same as the citation above; however, the article features headings. Using headings and the paragraph number within that section makes locating the quote an easy task. Notice that in this example there is a copyright date.

*Example in which there are no page numbers, there is an identified author, and there are headings:*

```
"A source of information is known to be scholarly when it pro-
vides references to the information presented" (Alexander &
Tate, 2009b, "Accuracy," section a, para. 1).
```

In this example the authors use section headings and then divide each section in lettered sub-sections. Notice both the section heading, "Accuracy," and the subsection, "section a" along with the paragraph number within section a are identified to make locating the quote easy.

***If the quote is 40 words or longer*** you will make what is called a block quotation. Start the block quotation on a new line; indent the entire quotation about 5 spaces from the left margin or a half-inch (generally your indentation for your block quotation should be the same as your paragraph indentation). With a block quote you do not use quotation marks. Notice in this example the writer begins in her own words and then uses a block quotation.

*Example:* There are many influences on built structures. This is true today, and it was true in the past.

```
One does not have to be a Marxist to see that the great castles
and cathedrals of the Middle Ages, the palaces and country hous-
es of later times, the parliaments and government buildings,
even the theatres and museums, were all (whatever else) blatant
expressions of authority and power and the desire to display
that power. (Sutton, 1999, p. 7)
```

Notice in the above example that the in-text citation is placed after the final punctuation mark. If your block quote is more than one paragraph, indent the first line of the second paragraph and all subsequent paragraphs five spaces from the new margin. (Note: generally, it is wise to avoid long quotations.)

***If specific facts or ideas are taken from a source*** include a text citation and always include the page number from which the facts were taken in the citation, even if you are paraphrasing the material. When citing specific facts or ideas, the citation is usually placed next to the sentence or sentences containing the facts. The in-text citation may occur at the end of a paragraph if all the information in that paragraph is from a single source as in the example below.

*Example:*

```
These interests led to the development of our purpose statement.
The purpose of this study was to determine how useful a quanti-
tative study of extant garments might be to the study of styles
worn in one region and to explore extant outdoor garments worn
by women in one state, Oregon, from 1880 to 1920. These dates
represent the years that settlement, town development, and com-
merce was being established in the Willamette Valley and East-
ern Oregon. Eastern Oregon was slower to develop due to climate,
```

terrain, transportation, and Native American relations (Brogan, 1977, pp. 48-59).

In the above example, the last two sentences paraphrase Brogan's work.

***Sometimes more than one reference is included in a citation*** to show the reader that multiple authors supported this idea or finding. When there are multiple works in a citation, place the authors in alphabetical order within the citation.

*Example:*

In the United States, upper class fashion leadership occurred in the 17th and 18th centuries for both genders and all age groups (Kidwell & Christman, 1974, p. 19; Sproles & Burns, 1994, p. 112).

***If you use the surname of an author as part of your narrative*** then place the citation immediately following the surname, generally using only the date in the citation.

*Example:*

Prown (1993) states that there are socio-cultural reasons behind why an object exists and exists in a particular style, shape, and material. This may be a result of tradition, contemporary attitudes and beliefs, and/or aspects related to the individual characteristics of the particular maker/designer. These attitudes and beliefs (world view) influenced both the maker and the consumer of the artifact.

If you ***use the surname of an author as part of your paraphrased narrative*** and ***later*** in the paragraph ***you quote from the author***, then place the year the author's work was published immediately following the author's name and place the page number of the quotation immediately following the quoted material.

*Example:*

In the book, *The End of Fashion: How Marketing Changed the Clothing Business Forever,* Teri Agins (1999) discusses how the fashion world changed at the end of the 20th century when the trickle-down process of fashion was disappearing and trickle-up and trickle-across fashion change was more common. She uses Isaac Mizrahi as an example at the beginning of her book. "There's no better example than Mizrahi to show what has been happening lately in the real world of fashion. It's not only the end of the millennium, but the end of fashion as we once knew it" (p. 6).

***For a work with two authors***, cite *both* surnames *every time* the reference occurs in the text.

*Example:*

Different types of customers prefer different types of fit (Johnson & Moore, 2001, p. 81).

***If there are three, four, or five authors***, the first reference citation should include all the authors' surnames; subsequent citations use only the surname of the first author followed by et al.

*Example:*

Really well written history of architecture books go beyond pure descriptive information. A well written text encourages "*seeing*. . . . Seeing requires proceeding beyond the image projected on the retina to a process of analysis and the making of critical judgments. This, in turn, calls for placing buildings in their various contexts" (Moffet, Fazio, & Wodehouse, 2004, p. 1). However, not only does a book need to be written in a certain way to enable "seeing," but also readers need to be ready to consider and think about what they are reading. They need "to enter the mind of the architect and to suspend modern biases so that we can evaluate the work as the product of a particular time and place" (Moffet et al., 2004, p. 1).

Notice also in the first quotation there are three spaced periods (e.g., . . .) known as ellipses. The ellipses tell the reader that the writer (you, not Moffet et al.) chose to quote only a selected portion of the entire sentence (or several sentences). The use of an ellipsis marks the omission of words from a quote. Do not use ellipses at the beginning or at the end of a quote; use them only if you omit part of the middle of the quote.

***If a work has six or more authors***, only the surname of the first author is used. For example, if you use a work published in 2002 by the authors Agin, Brown, Clark, Durke, Eel, Ford, and Graham, the in-text citation would be (Agin, et al., 2002). All of the authors' names will appear in the reference list.

***When there is no author***, cite the first two or three words of the title and the year of publication. Use this type of citation for newspaper articles, magazine articles, brochures, Web pages, and so forth that have no identified author. Use quotation marks around the title of articles, book chapters, or Web pages. If you are using the title of a book, brochure, magazine, periodical, a report, or an entire Web site, italicize the title.

*Example of an article with no identified author:*

It has been said that "referencing helps create a map of knowledge" ("Why do we," 2013, para. 1).

*Example of a book with no identified author:*

Studying images of English Tudor manors, one can see that diamond-shaped panes were typical to that time period while window shapes might be similar to Gothic pointed windows or simple rectangles (*The Domestic Architecture*, 1923).

Note that when using Web sources, it may appear there is no author because often there is no name at the top of the page. However, a number of authors will put their name at the bottom of the page or on the home page. So it is important that you explore the site to determine the author's name. The same is true for the copyright date of most Web pages; the copyright date is not always easy to find. But it is important to search for the date. Start by looking at the bottom of the page, and if no date appears there next go to the home page or look to see if there is a link to "copyright" or "copyright information."

***Nontraditional sources of information*** such as *Facebook* and *Twitter*. It is possible to adapt most forms of communication to the APA style; you need to keep in mind the basic information that is required. Though citing and referencing Facebook and Twitter are not mentioned in the APA manual, if you go to the APA Style Web site there is discussion of using Facebook and Twitter (http://blog.apastyle.org/apastyle/2009/10/how-to-cite-twitter-and-facebook-part-i.html). The current rule for Facebook and Twitter is that you must provide a citation as you do with any source other than your own ideas, but you do not need to provide a reference if you are referring to an entire site.

"To cite a Twitter or Facebook feed as a whole or to discuss it in general, it is sufficient to give the site URL in text, inside parentheses" (Lee, 2009, Oct. 23, para. 2). By providing the URL for the Facebook or Twitter source, you do not need a reference in your reference list.

For a specific post or feed your citation for Facebook or Twitter should contain the author or the feed and the date (Author, date) or if no author the first few words of the title and the date (Title of the Feed, date) (Lee, 2009, Oct. 26). For more information go to *How to Cite Twitter and Facebook, Part II: Reference List Entries and In-Text Citations* (http://blog.apastyle.org/apastyle/2009/10/how-to-cite-twitter-and-facebook-part-ii.html). You will need a reference for specific posts or feeds.

If you use *Pinterest* as a resource remember that a large majority of the "pins" are not original to the specific Pinterest site. Thus, you need to check the source of the information found on any Pinterest site. If it is not original to the Pinterest board creator you will need to search out the original source and then cite within the body of your paper from the original source. If the information you wish to cite is original to the Pinterest board creator then use the individual's last name or screen name and the date of the Pinterest posting. Use "n.d." only if no date for the board can be found. Use the screen name only if the individual's family name is not available. If you have a Pinterest text citation you will also need a reference to the posting in your reference list. See the reference discussion below in the Reference List Format Guidelines section.

***Personal communications*** such as class lectures, interviews, and other face-to-face communication should be cited in your text. Personal communication also includes telephone conversations, private letters, and email messages. If you quote the individual instead of paraphrasing the comments use quotation marks. "Because they do not provide recoverable data, personal communications are not included in the reference list" (*Publication Manual,* 2010, p. 179). Your personal communication text citation looks like this

```
E. L. Pedersen (personal communication, June 3, 2013).

(K. Mullet, personal communication, June 3, 2013).
```

Always include the initials of the first and middle name (middle name initials, if available). Some types of personal communication are recoverable and in that case the citation would also require a reference in the reference list. Also, check with your instructor in case there is a different requirement for personal communication citation.

## Illustration Captions and References

All illustrations should have captions. *The purpose of the caption* is to provide an explanation or description of the illustration. While you do not want a long explanation in a caption, one that is too brief, such as two or three words, is not useful. Captions are placed below the illustration immediately prior to the illustration reference. See examples below.

In the APA Style, the term "figure" is used for illustrations. These illustrations may be graphs, charts, drawings, photographs, or other types of illustrations. In many APA style publications, figures are developed for and/or relate to a particular research study that is being reported. The information provided here is an adaptation from APA specifications on the use of figures especially those that require a reference.

Each figure (illustration) has a figure number and title placed above the illustration (at the top of the page if the illustration is the only item on the page). Each illustration should be given a sequential "Figure" number (i.e., Figure 1, Figure 2, etc.). The illustration is placed just below the title and is followed by the caption, which ends with the reference. Note the word *reference*; citations are NOT used with figures. Though different from the list of references at the back of the paper, a figure caption contains complete reference information. The illustration reference follows the illustration caption and begins with "From" or "Adapted from" followed by the reference information.

The examples provided below are examples of how the full references used with illustrations are different from those you put in your list of references at the end of your paper. The *basic format for illustration references* is title of the work (article, book, Web page), author's name (initials of first name/middle name followed by the last name), and date. The remaining information in the illustration reference varies depending upon the type of source. If elements for the reference are missing, cite what information you have. Remember with Web illustrations to spend some time searching for information as the date and author/illustrator's name are not always immediately obvious. If the date is missing use "n.d." instead, but be sure first to verify that the date is truly missing. The last piece of information should be about the copyright holder or the maker of the illustration. See examples below

*Illustration found in an article:*

Caption would be here. From "Title of Article" by A. N. Author, year of publication, *Title of Journal, volume no.*, page no. Copyright [Year] by Name of Copyright Holder.[1]

Caption would be here. From "Stella Blum Grant Report: Idle Hands and Empty Pockets: Postures of Leisure," by H. Carlson, 2008-2009, *Dress, 35,* p. 20. Copyright 2008-2009 by *Dress*.

**Figure 1**. Caption and Reference Example for an Illustration in an Article

Elaine Pedersen and Kathy Mullet studying tour guide book in Rome. From "College Faculty Abroad: How Faculty Use Their International Trips to Enhance Their Teaching," by J. Instructor, 2013, *Teaching Trips for Faculty, 1*, p. 1–5.[2] Copyright 2013 by *Teaching Tips for Faculty*. Photograph by Ron Mullet.

*Illustration found in a book:*

Caption would be here. From *Title of Book* by N. A. Author, year of publication, City of Publication, State: Publisher, p. x. Copyright [Year] by the Name of Copyright Holder [usually the publisher].

Classical ornamentation: Egg and Dart; Fret. From *The Study of Interior Decoration* by A. Jackson and B. Jackson, 1928, Garden City, NY: Doubleday, Doran & Company, Inc. Copyright 1928 by Doubleday, Doran & Company, Inc.

**Figure 2.** Caption and Reference Example for an Illustration in a Book

Elaine and Marilyn Pedersen in 1953 in Juneau, Alaska wearing winter attire. From *Winter Clothing for Children in the 1950s* by I. M. Author, 1970, Nowhere, IZ: Nothing Publisher, Inc.[3] Copyright 1970 by Nothing Publisher, Inc.

*Illustration found on-line in a Web site:*

If an author is identified:

Caption would be here. From "Title of web section" by N. A. Author, year of publication, *Title of Web document*, Retrieved from XXXX Website: http://www.xxxxxxxx.xxx Copyright [year] by Name of Copyright Holder.

If there is no identified author:

Notice the full use of tile in this illustration of a bathroom. From "A Contemporary Tiled Bathroom" by Better Homes and Gardens, 2013, *Better Homes & Gardens Network*, Meredith Corporation, Retrieved from http://www.bhg.com/bathroom/decorating/modern/contemporary-tiled-bath/ Copyright 2013 by Meredith Corporation.[4]

Notice for this illustration reference the "author" is a company, Better Homes and Gardens.

This is an example of an extra wide chair. From "Daphne Chair & A Half" by La_Z-Boy, Inc, 2013, *LAZBOY: Live life comfortably*, Retrieved from http://www.la-z-boy.com/Product/80-6949/Daphne-Fabric-Chair/ Copyright 2013 by La-Z-Boy, Inc.

Note: for both the La-Z-Boy and Better Homes and Gardens examples these are illustrations that are copyrighted, and if you use a copyrighted illustration for any type of work beyond a class assignment you should seek permission for use from the holder of the copyright.

**Figure 3.** Caption and Reference Example for a Web Illustration

The Jefferson Memorial in Washington DC is a good example of the influence of classical architecture on government buildings. This memorial, a neoclassical building honoring Thomas Jefferson as a founding father and the third President of the United States, was built between 1939 and 1943. From "135 Photos of United States, North America: United States," by Central Intelligence Agency, 2013, *The World Factbook,* Retrieved from https://www.cia.gov/library/publications/the-world-factbook/geos/us.html Public Domain 2013 Central Intelligence Agency, U.S. Government, Image US_028.

Note: in the above example the image comes from a U.S. Government Web site in which public domain images are available. This is indicated at the end of the illustration reference where "Public Domain" is used instead of "Copyright." Other government public domain Web sites are NASA and USGS. Note that "Image US_028" has been added at the end of the illustration reference as the URL leads the reader to the general site in which the individual images may be viewed.

*Illustrations that you make:*

For a number of your projects you may be the illustrator. Here are two examples of what the figure title, caption, and reference would look like.

**Figure 4.** Socio-Cultural Influences on the Near Environment

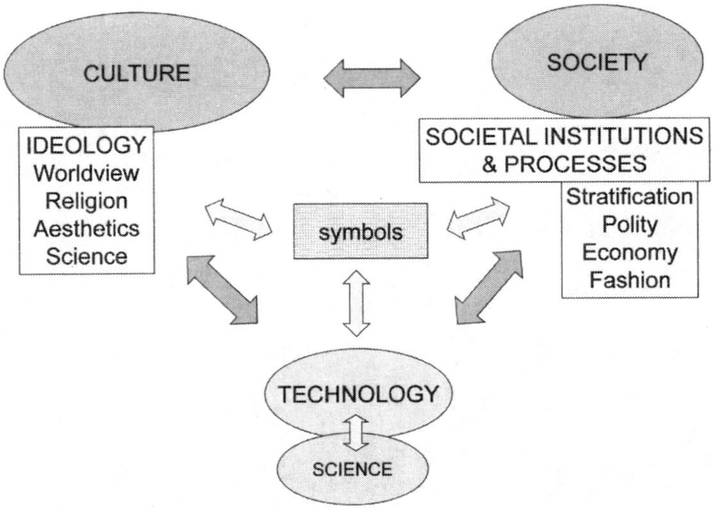


Framework for the History of the Near Environment courses in the School of Design and Human Environment. From DHE 461 and 462, by E. L. Pedersen.

**Figure 5.** Example of an Entablature

The photograph shows the entablature found on Milam Hall at Oregon State University. This entablature has been modified from the traditional ancient Greek and Roman entablatures. By E. L. Pedersen.

## Reference List Format Guidelines

Create a list of your references at the end of your paper. This list includes all of the sources you have cited from within the text of your paper. The reference list at the end of your paper documents your paper and provides the information necessary for the reader to identify and find each source. With the APA style you include only the sources that were cited in your paper. List references in alphabetical order by authors' names (last name, first). There are several types of material that are cited only in your text and are not included in your reference list: "references to classical works such as the Bible and the Qur'an" (*Publication Manual*, 2010, p. 174), personal communication references, and Facebook and Twitter references when you are referring to the entire feed (specific feeds or posts should be in your reference list).

A large body of information is now available via electronic retrieval. The basic rule in formatting a reference for a piece of information that you have retrieved or that can be retrieved electronically is to "include the same elements, in the same order, as you would for a reference to a fixed-media source and add as much electronic retrieval information as needed for others to locate the sources you cited" (*Publication Manual*, 2010, p. 187). See examples below.

Today, many journal articles have DOI (digital object identifiers); this is also true of other electronically available sources. When you are writing down the reference information for an electronic source look for the DOI. You may find it in the following places: it may be located in the original database listing, it may be listed at the top of the first page of an article, in a side margin of the first page, it may be located at the bottom of the first page of the article, or on a book's copyright page. If you cannot locate the DOI be sure to include the URL for the electronic source so that others can locate this source.

> Because one purpose of listing references is to enable readers to retrieve and use the sources, most entries contain the following elements: author, year of publication, title, and publishing or retrieval data – all the information necessary for unique identification and library search. (*Publication Manual,* 2010, p. 193)

If the source does not have an author, list the title first. When the date is missing from the publication, use the abbreviation n.d. in parentheses to indicate "no date."

The following are examples of the variety of different types of sources that might be included in your reference list. See your instructor if you do not find an example for the type of reference source you have used; you can also go to the *Publication Manual of the American Psychological Association* (2010), or visit www.apastyle.org. Do note that APA differentiates in reference style between articles from scholarly journals and those from magazines or popular source periodicals.

Notice below that there are differences among different types of periodicals. Magazine articles and scholarly journal articles are referenced somewhat differently. Thus you will need to be able to recognize what type of article you are using. Scholarly sources, including scholarly journals, typically present information formally and often have article abstracts. The work that is reported is original research or other types of scholarly work completed by academics (university faculty). Scholarly work will contain text citations and reference lists (Hacker & Sommers, 2011). Written work in a popular source may or may not acknowledge the writer. Though some academics write in popular sources, more often the author is a staff member of the magazine. The content of the article will not be original but may include summaries of research findings depending upon the topic of the article. It is extremely rare to find references or text citations in popular writing. Instead sources are acknowledged within a sentence. The reason that faculty often require students to use scholarly writing instead of popular press writing is because the work that is found in popular writing is secondary or tertiary source material. Scholarly writing is primary source material.

## Research or scholarly journal article

As discussed above, research journal articles or scholarly articles are those that are written by scholars. These scholars are often university faculty. A research or scholarly journal article is one that has been written by an individual who used appropriate research methods to make an original scholarly discovery. Most research or scholarly journal articles have been reviewed by other scholars to determine if the article is of sufficient quality and merit for publication. The basic format for a research journal article reference is as follows:

Author's last name, First initial or initials. (year of publication). Title of article. *Title of Journal, volume number*, starting page number-ending page number. Digital object identifier

OR

Author, X. X. (2010). Title of article. *Title of Journal, XX*, 11-12. doi: xx.xxxx/namenumber.xxxxxxx

Author, X. X. (2010). Title of article:Subtitle of article. *Title of Journal, XX*, 11-12. doi: xx.xxxx/namenumber.xxxxxxx

The title of the article should have the first letter of the first word capitalized only. For titles with subtitles, a colon [:] is used between the title and the subtitle; the first letter of the first word of *both* the title and subtitle is capitalized. The title of the journal and the volume number of the journal are in italics.

As discussed, because many scholarly journal articles are now available online, it is important to include in the reference the digital object identifier (DOI) if available. "The DOIs in the reference list function as links to the content you are referencing" (*Publication Manual,* 2010, p. 189).

### *Journal article with DOI*

Huang, J. (2006). Thermal parameters for assessing thermal properties of clothing. *Journal of Thermal Biology, 31*, 461-466. doi: 10.1016/j.jtherbio.2006.03.001

### *Journal article without DOI (no DOI is available)*

Pedersen, E., & Lawson, L. (1995). The Logan Knitting Mills, 1949 to 1980: Perspectives on success and failure. *Ars Textrina, 23*, 143-156.

## Magazine article

As discussed above, magazine articles are written by the staff of the magazine (or a paid author), and the articles are written for the general public. Another type of magazine is the trade publication. Trade publications are written for members of a particular part of industry (i.e., *Contract* and *Designers West* are written for professional interior designers). Because the reporting of research findings is secondary or tertiary, generally the reporting of research findings is of a lower quality than is found in research or scholarly journal articles.

### *Hard copy magazine article*

The basic format for a magazine article reference is as follows:

Author's last name, first initial or initials. (year of publication, month of publication). Title of article. *Title of Magazine, volume number*(issue number), starting page number-ending page number (or if article does not have continuous pages a list of pages in consecutive order).

OR

Marcoux, S. T. (2013, August). Super Saver. *Better Homes and Gardens, 91*(8), 38-44.

OR

Trends worth trying 5/12. (May, 2013). *Real Simple*, 39-40, 42, 44, 46, 48.

Note: this last example shows you both how to reference a magazine article where no author is indicated and when advertising pages interrupt the article content, and there are no continuous page numbers.

### *Online magazine article*

The basic format for an online magazine article reference is the same as above. At the end of the reference add "Retrieved from" and add the URL.

Nelson, J. (2013, August 30). Announcing GQ's new special edition: What to wear now. *GQ*. Retrieved from http://www.gq.com/magazine/201309/what-to-wear-now/jim-nelson-what-to-wear-now-2013

## Newspaper article

Newspaper articles may or may not have recognized authors. The basic reference style is very similar to the magazine article reference style. If there is no author, put the title of the article first followed by the publication date as shown below; then, put the title of the newspaper followed by the page numbers (or URL if it is an online newspaper).

### *Hard copy newspaper article*

The basic style is:

Author's last name, first initial or initials. (year of publication, month and day of publication). Title of article. *Title of Newspaper,* pp. starting page number-ending page number (or if article does not have continuous pages a list of pages in consecutive order).

OR

Lockwood, L. (1987, June 1). Designer licensing—The survivors. *Women's Wear Daily,* p. 10.

OR

Textile-apparel imports leap in September. (1981, October 27). *Women's Wear Daily*, pp. 19, 23.

Note the use of "p" and "pp." preceding the actual page numbers for the article. This is different from the magazine reference style.

### *Online newspaper article*

The basic format for an online newspaper article reference is the same as above. At the end of the reference, add "Retrieved from" and add the URL.

Hall, B. (2013, July 10). Clock ticking on OSU board decision. *Corvallis Gazette Times*. Retrieved from http://www.gazettetimes.com/news/local/clock-ticking-on-osu-board-decision/article_2565c472-e8da-11e2-8917-0019bb2963f4.html

## Entire books

If your source is a book written by the same author or authors throughout (as opposed to each chapter being written by a different author) you will use the following style.

Author's last name, first initial. (Year of publication.) *Title of the book*. City, State of publisher (using postal abbreviations for the state): Name of Publisher.

If the book was published outside the United States then use the city and name of the country in which the book was published.

### *One author*

Barker, C. (2012). *Photoshop down & dirty tricks for designers*. Berkeley, CA: New Riders.

### *Two authors*

Piotrowski, C. M., & Rogers, E. A. (2007). *Designing commercial interiors*. Hoboken, NJ: Wiley.

### *Three authors, edition other than the first*

Burns, L. D., Mullet, K. K., & Bryant, N. O. (2011). *The business of fashion: Designing, manufacturing, and marketing* (4th ed.). New York, NY: Fairchild.

### *Author and translator; published outside of the United States*

Chenoune, F. (1993). *A history of men's fashion* (D. Dusinberre, Trans.). Paris, France: Flammarion.

### *Book with title and subtitle*

Scalise, C. M. (2008). *Interior design illustrated: Marker and water-color techniques*. New York, NY: Fairchild.

### *Book with an editor*

Arthur, L. B. (Ed.). (2000). *Undressing religion: Commitment and con-version from a cross-cultural perspective*. Oxford, England: Berg.

### Article or chapter in an edited book

As mentioned above, sometimes each chapter in a book is written by a different author. In that case the book has an editor. Sometimes you will reference the entire book (see above "Book with an editor"), but more often you need to reference one of the chapters. To do so you will use the following style.

Chapter author's last name, first initial. (Year of publication.) Title of the article. First initial of editor's name, Editor's last name (Ed.). *Title of the Book* (page numbers of the chapter). City, State of publisher (using postal abbreviations for the state): Name of Publisher.

### *One chapter author, two editors of edited book*

McCracken, G. (2007). The fashion system. In W. Welters & A. Lillethun (Eds.). *The Fashion Reader* (pp. 90-92). Oxford, England: Berg.

### *Two chapter authors, two editors of edited book*

Lang, K., & Lang, G. E.  (2007). The power of fashion. In W. Welters & A. Lillethun (Eds.). *The Fashion Reader* (pp. 77-82). Oxford, England: Berg.

### *Two chapter authors, two editors, multivolume book*

Carter, T., & Herman, B. L. (1991). Introduction: Toward a new archi-tectural history.  In T. Carter and B. L. Herman (Eds.). *Perspec-tives in Vernacular Architecture (Vol.IV)*. (pp. 1-6). Columbia, MO: University of Missouri Press.

Note that in the above example the editors of the book wrote one of the chapters in the book. In this case their names are listed two times, once as chapter authors and once as editors of the book. Notice also that for the chapter title only the first letter of the first word is capitalized, while each of the first letters of the words in the book title is capitalized (excepting words like "the," "a," "of," etc.).

## Articles or chapters in special publications

Special publications are typically publications that professional organizations produce. These may include conference proceedings, monographs, and publications by a variety of organizations that are not typically publishers. The basic format follows that of either a book or a chapter in an edited book. Here are some examples.

### *Conference proceedings with two authors and no identified editor*

Memken, J. A., & Schertz, A. (1990). An historic study of the American foursquare: Implications for historic preservation. In *Silver Anniversary: Golden Opportunity* (pp. 118-136). Columbia, MO: American Association of Housing Educators.

### *Conference proceedings with two authors and one editor*

Paff, J. L., & Lakner, H. B. (1995). Dress and the female gender role in magazine advertisements of 1950-1994: A content analysis. In C. M. Ladisch (Ed.). *ITAA Proceedings: Proceedings of the International Textiles and Apparel Association* (p. 121). Boulder, CO: ITAA, Inc.

### *Online conference paper*

Cho, H. J., & Jin, B. (2012, November). *An application of Uppsala Model to internationalization of U.S. fashion companies: The cases of Tiffany & Co. and Polo Ralph Lauren in Japan.* Paper presented at the International Textiles and Apparel Conference, Honolulu, HI. Abstract retrieved from http://cdm16001.contentdm.oclc.org/cdm/compoundobject/collection/p16001coll5/id/12751

Notice that the title of the abstract is in italics.

### *Professional organization monograph*

Gunn, V. (1991). A case for the historical method in clothing and textiles research. In S. B. Kaiser & M. L. Damhorst (Eds.). *Critical Linkages in Textiles and Clothing Subject Matter: Theory, Method and Practice: ITAA Special Publication #4* (pp. 139-149). Boulder, CO: International Textile and Apparel Association, Inc.

### *Academic department publication, one author, several editors*

Blackman, Margaret B. (1986). Visual ethnohistory: Photographs in the study of culture history. In D. Wiedman (Guest Ed.) & V. H. Sutlive, N. Altshuter, M. D. Zemora, & V. Kerns (Series Ed.). *Ethnohistory: A Researcher's Guide. Studies in Third World Societies Publication Number Thirty Five* (pp. 137-166). Williamsburg, VA: Department of Anthropology, College of William and Mary.

Note: The above reference is also an example of an article published in a reoccurring series of publications (*Studies in Third World Societies*). This example shows you how to note a guest editor and series editor(s) as well as a publication that is numbered. Usually either a guest editor or a series editor will be identified.

## Other types of publications

Generally, the same basic format is used for all publications (i.e., Author, Title, Location of publishing institution, Name of publishing institution OR Author, Title of Chapter, Editor, Title of edited publication, Location of publishing institution, Publishing institution.). For all of these references generally you would use the author's name and year of publication in the text citation as you do with books and articles unless noted otherwise. Here are some reference examples of other types of "publications."

### *Corporation annual report*

NIKE, Incorporated. (2000). *NIKE, Incorporated Annual Report*. Beaverton, OR: Author.

Notice that when the "author" is the same entity as the publisher, you do not have to repeat the name. You can instead state "author" immediately following the location of the "publisher."

### *Technical and research reports*

Wilkie, W. L. (1975). *How consumers use product information.* (Report prepared for the National Science Foundation). Washington DC: U. S. Government Printing Office.

OR

University of Michigan. (2012, November). *Examining the disadvantaged business enterprise (DBE) program* (Accession No. PB2013-108894, NTIS Issue No. 1320) [CD]. Washington, DC: Federal Highway Administration, U.S. Department of Transportation.

Note that there is a "corporate" or in this case a university author. Note also the [CD] in this reference. Brackets are used to tell the reader the type of "publication" if it is for the "identification and retrieval" of the resource (*Publication* Manual, 2010, p. 186). In this example the use of brackets and "CD" informs the reader that this publication is available via compact disc.

OR

Adamski, M., Elliott, C., & Simon-Brown, V. (2011). Living sustainably: It's your choice (EC 1614-E). Corvallis, OR: Oregon State University Extension Service. Retrieved from https://ir.library.oregonstate.edu/xmlui/bitstream/handle/1957/26069/ec1614.pdf

As mentioned earlier, sometimes it is necessary with a Web resource to hunt for reference information. With the above reference the authors' names were not placed on the title page or the first "inside" page of the publication. Instead they were listed on the last page.

### *Unpublished doctoral dissertations and master's theses, print version*

Christel, D. A. (2010). *Perceived comfort of three styles of men's running pants* (Doctoral dissertation). Oregon State University, Corvallis, OR.

### *Unpublished doctoral dissertations and master's theses, electronic version*

Christel, D. A. (2010). *Perceived comfort of three styles of men's running pants* (Doctoral dissertation). Retrieved from http://ir.library.oregonstate.edu/xmlui/bitstream/handle/1957/16552/ChristelDeborahA2010.pdf?sequence=1

***Motion Picture:*** When referencing a video the format is

Producer, A. A. (Producer), & Director, B. B. (Director). (Year). *Title of motion picture* [Motion picture/DVD]. Country of origin: Studio.

OR

Telling, L. (Producer, Director). (2007). *Addicted to cheap shopping?* (DVD]. United States: Films for the Humanities & Sciences.

OR

Gilliam, J., & Smith, D. (Producers), & Greenwald, R. (Director). (2005). *Wal*Mart: The high cost of low price* [DVD]. United States: Brave New Films.

***Music Recording:*** When referencing a music recording the format is

Writer, A. (Copyright year). Title of song [Recorded by B. B. Artist if different from writer]. On *Title of album* [Medium of recording: CD, record, cassette, etc.] Location: Label. (Date of recording if different from song copyright date)

OR

Joel, B. (2001). It's still rock and roll to me. On *The essential Billy Joel* [CD] New York, NY: Columbia/Sony Music Entertainment, Inc.

### *YouTube videos*

When referencing a YouTube video, try to find the real name of the person and then use both the real name and the screen name in the reference. Having the real name is useful if this individual has authored other types of work. However, if the real name is not available, then you will use only the screen name. For the in-text citation always use the real name and year of the video; however, if only the screen name is available, use the screen name and year of the video. An example would be using the *Interior Design* video referenced below (e.g., Hooyaiyei, 2006).

The format is as follows when both names are available

Author, A. A. [Screen name]. (year, month day). *Title of video* [Video file]. Retrieved from http://xxxx

OR

Giannini, F. [FatalefashionIll]. (2013, February 20). *Gucci/Fall Winter 2013/2014 Full Fashion Show/Exclusive* [Video file]. Retrieved from http://www.youtube.com/watch?v=2hnmFQHwKMA

When only the screen name is available the format is

Screen name. (year, month day). *Title of video* [Video file]. Retrieved from http://xxxx

OR

Hooyaiyei. (2006, December 31). *Interior design* [Video file]. Retrieved from http://www.youtube.com/watch?v=Eb--aXUj5wE

### *Blogs*

The basic APA style is also mostly followed in referencing a blog. The format is

Author, A. A. (year of publication). Title of the post. *Title of the blog* [web log]. Retrieved month, year, from http://xxxx

OR

Brisbane, T. (2013). Preparing for decoration show. *Thea & Sami: The studio blog* [web log]. Retrieved July, 2013, from http://theaandsami.blogspot.com/

Below is an example where there is no author, similar to above (for articles); the title of the post is placed where the author's name would be, and the first two or three words of the title would be used in place of an author's name in the in-text citation (Kate Spade, 2013):

Kate Spade Floral Dresses - Summer 2013 (2013). *Textile Source Blog* [web log]. Retrieved July, 2013, from http://textile-blog.com/

### *Facebook and Twitter*

As mentioned under text citations it is possible to adapt most forms of communication to the APA style; you need to keep in mind the basic information that is required. Though citing and referencing Facebook and Twitter are not mentioned in the APA manual, if you go to the APA Style Web site there is discussion of these rules (http://blog.apastyle.org/apastyle/2009/10/how-to-cite-twitter-and-facebook-part-i.html and http://blog.apastyle.org/apastyle/2009/10/how-to-cite-twitter-and-facebook-part-ii.html).

The current rule for Facebook and Twitter is that you must provide a citation as you do with any source, but if you cite the entire feed you do not need to provide a reference (Lee, 2009, Oct. 23). See Facebook and Twitter above under "Citations." However, if you cite a specific feed or post then you will need a reference (Lee, 2009, Oct. 26). Twitter and Facebook references for a specific feed follows the general APA style:

```
Author of post or full title/post. (year, month day). Title of Twitter
      or Facebook feed [Twitter Post or Facebook Post]. Retrieved from
      http://URL for specific feed
```

OR

```
Costume Society. (2013, August 29). Deadline for our National sympo-
      sium call for papers approaches: Don't forget to send in your
      abstracts! http://ow.ly/oiQ8Q [Twitter Post]. Retrieved from
      https://twitter.com/CostumeSociety/status/373105786052157440
```

OR

```
Costume Society of America. (2013, August 27). The early bird deadline
      for Uncommon Beauty, CSA Midwest Symposium is extended to
      August 29. Don't delay, register and book your hotel today!
      http://ow.ly/oiPOz [Facebook post]. Retrieved from https://www.
      facebook.com/costumesocietyofamerica/posts/10151816643414138
```

OR

```
Do you have #APAStyle questions? Our style blog has the answers! Browse
      or search posts from style experts at blog.apastsyle.org (2013,
      Sept 6). APA Style@APA_Style [Twitter Post]. Retrieved from
      https://twitter.com/APA_Style
```

Note—when the post includes a URL include that as you see above, just before [Twitter Post]. Also notice, if there is no author you put the entire Tweet before the date of the post.

OR

```
Kevin Bieksa (2013, Sept. 7). Met a lot of great Canuck fans in The
      Rupe! We are very surprised and overwhelmed with the support up
      here. Couple beauties too eh. . . [Twitter Post]. Retrieved from
      https://twitter.com/kbieksa3
```

If a specific author's name is provided write the name as spelled/written; this ensures the accuracy for someone trying to retrieve the post. Alphabetize under the order given in the post. For example, Kevin Bieksa and not Bieksa, K. If you need to differentiate among posts from the same person on the same date then use an "a" or "b" after the year and place them in chronological order (e.g., 2013a, 2013b). If the title of the entire feed is long you might use a truncated version; if the URL for the entire feed is included as part of the title you may include it in your reference.

### *Pinterest*

As discussed above in the In-text citation section the majority of Pinterest pins are not original to the specific Pinterest sites. To use the information correctly you need to locate the original source and cite and reference from that original source. In the case of information original to the Pinterest board creator always use the individual's family name and initials of the first and middle names if available. If there is a screen name in addition put the screen name in brackets and be sure to note your source is from Pinterest in brackets after the title of the posting.

`Author, A. A. [Screen name]. (year, month day).` *`Pinterest title`* `[Pinterest Post]. Retrieved from http://xxxx`

*Endnotes*

1. Copyright may be held by the individual who made the illustration, the journal, or a specific organization.
2. This is not a real journal; it was "made up" to use as an example.
3. This is not a real book; it was made up to use as an example.
4. For this illustration the copyright information, the year and the holder of the copyright, were available at the bottom of the Web page.

CHAPTER FOUR

# Evaluating Print and Web Resources

In the majority of the formal writing you will do as a student, you will be asked to seek sources, related to the topic of the writing assignment, that provide additional information to that found in your textbooks. Generally, most of your sources will be print and Web resources. Print sources include articles in magazines, journals, and edited and authored books, along with textbooks. Other print sources that you may use include newspapers, museum catalogues, pamphlets, and brochures. In the last several decades, individuals have also begun to find information on the World Wide Web. However, even today, there are some disciplines and some topics that are not well represented online; sometimes the best, most reliable sources are print sources. Be sure to ask your instructor about the best location for sources on your topic.

Wherever you find information relevant to your topic, it is important that you are critical about the usefulness, potential accuracy, authority, objectivity, currency, and coverage of that information before you incorporate it into your written assignment.[1] Using poor or inaccurate information will lower the quality of your work. There are criteria that you can use to help you determine the usefulness of your resources. Some of the criteria apply more to written print information while other criteria are more specific to Web resources.

## Accuracy

A key question to ask about any source of information concerns whether the information is *reliable* and *free from error*. Accuracy often relates to what source(s) the author used and how well the information was interpreted. Many reliable print resources include a discussion of how the information was gathered and analyzed. In books this information may be found in the preface or sometimes in an appendix. In research and other scholarly articles there will usually be a methods section discussing the collection of data.[2] With books or other sources, it is also useful to determine if the book has been self-published. A self-published source is not necessarily inaccurate; however, when an author uses a known publisher the publisher will set standards and have the book reviewed for accuracy and other quality characteristics. This does not always occur with a self-published work. You will need to look very carefully at the credentials of the author(s) of a self-published work to determine if the work is of an adequate quality for your purpose.

A discussion of the author's information sources or data collection procedures may or may not be available in Web resources. Lack of information about the author's sources may indicate poor quality or inaccuracy. Remember when considering Web resources that almost anyone can "put something out" on the Web. Availability of information on the Web **does not** mean the information is accurate.

When *evaluating a Web resource* check to see if the sources for the factual information are listed ("Accuracy," 2012, para. 1):

- Can the facts in a Web resource be verified in another source?
- Is there a reference list or are sources named within the work?
- If sources are listed within the work, do the sources/references appear to be scholarly and reliable?
- Are there grammatical, spelling, or other typographical errors? These errors show a lack of quality control and, obviously, can create inaccuracy in the information.
- Are you finding vague or sweeping generalizations and anonymity of the writer(s)?
- Does the author appear biased about the subject? Bias may affect accuracy. For example, some news reports tend toward the more conservative right while others lean more toward the liberal left when reporting and interpreting events. Often bias can be located by the use of certain words.

For a book, look at the book reviews to determine if reviewers thought the author was biased. In order to find book reviews, contact a librarian or search the Web. Be sure to note the source of the book review as reviewers themselves may be biased (Hacker & Sommers, 2011, pp. 353–354). Do not use a book that has many negative reviews.

Bias, in any source, may be religious, political, or related to a particular special interest such as gun rights, medical decisions, and so forth. In evaluating for bias, check to see if more than one viewpoint is presented. And if several views are presented, are they treated equally? (Hacker & Sommers, 2011, pp. 353–354).

Other indicators of accuracy are authority, objectivity, currency, and coverage. Each of these characteristics is discussed below.

## Authority/Authorship/Sponsorship

Knowing who wrote your source and/or sponsored the source is a most important criteria for evaluating a resource. In evaluating authority, consider the author's qualifications or expertise for discussing the subject about which he/she has written. Check the reliability of the information.

When evaluating a book author, consider the publisher's or organization's reputation for books on this subject. Some book publishers do include information on the author's credentials. In journal articles, often the author's scholarly affiliations will be listed. Unfortunately, this information is not always readily available for all print resources, and it is less available for Web resources (Alexander & Tate, 2009c; "Authorship and," 1995–2013, para. 1; Harris, 2010).

"Authorship and affiliations are difficult to determine on the Internet. Some sites may have author and sponsorship listed, but many do not" ("Authorship and," 1995-2013, para. 2). Regarding *Web sources*, ask:

- Does the resource have "a reputable organization or expert behind it" ? ("Authority," 2013, para. 3).
    - Look at the Web site's URL. It can suggest an affiliation with a reputable organization such as a university, government, or non-profit organization (e.g., edu, gov, org) ("Authority," 2012, para. 3).[3]
    - Look at how others discuss or refer to the organization. Use library databases to search for works containing discussions of the organization (Alexandar & Tate, 2009c).
- Have references for the work been given?
- Is contact information for the author available? ("Authority," 2013, para. 4, 5).

Stay away from Web resources for which you cannot determine the authorship or where there is no indication of the authority of the author regarding the subject he/she is discussing.

## Locating a Web author

Try to determine the author's education, training, experience, reputation, and current position. One can "try a Google search to find out more information about the author" ("Who is the," 2013, para. 2). Sometimes in Web resources it is difficult to determine who the author is. When the author's name is not at the top of the Web page, look at the document footer. Another location to check is the home page of the Web site. The home page is also where, if it is available, the institution to which the individual is connected will be listed along with the date of creation and/or revision.

## Questions to ask about a Web author

When information is available on the author, consider the following:

- Is the author the original creator of the information?
- Is the author a university faculty member or a professional representing some other quality institution?
- Is the institution with which the author is affiliated a national institution?
- Does the author have a history of writing on the topic? This would indicate a depth of knowledge, unless each publication repeats information from the last or other publications.
- Has the author published his/her works in reputable scholarly journals or written books published by reputable publishers?

Knowledge of the author's educational and/or occupational background may help in determining the reliability of the information. When an individual is a university faculty member, that is usually an indicator of expertise. University faculty are qualified to write about their field of knowledge. Ask yourself if this information you locate on the author provides the necessary qualifications to write on the topic of your research. If you are not sure of the individual's expertise, ask your instructor.

## Information on a Web author is not available

Sometimes you will not be able to locate information about a Web author. This does not always indicate a suspicious source. When information on a Web author is not available, ask:

- Is the Web site linked to another document that you trust?
- If the author's name is available but no other information is provided, is the address, telephone number, or email address for the author listed? If so, you can request information on the author's background and additional completed work.
- Can you locate information on the author using a search engine?
- Does a header or footer show affiliation with a larger Web site, perhaps part of an institutional setting? The URL may also give a clue as to the publishing body. (Alexander & Tate, 2009c, section a, para. 3)

If you need to find information on an organization or institution that appears to be hosting or affiliated with the site you are examining, you should investigate the organization or institution. To do this, go back to the root address. Using a site on Italian Renaissance architecture as an example (http://www.metmuseum.org/toah/hd/itar/hd_itar.htm), you can go back to http://www.metmuseum.org and learn that this resource is part of the Metropolitan Museum of Art in New York City; this is a well-respected source for history of material culture such as architecture (Alexander & Tate, 2009c).

## Objectivity

Try to determine whether the resource has been written from an objective perspective. Every written resource is influenced, whether slightly or highly, by the author's opinions, experiences, and education. You want to remember that resources represent a writer's viewpoint. Facts, themselves, represent a particular author's choices and ideas about what a fact is. If the author(s) appears to be trying to sway your opinion on the subject, this is an example of a *biased resource*. Be aware that at least some Web authors use the Web as a soapbox and often there is more biased information available on the Web on certain topics than there is objective information available. You may wish to ask yourself the following questions:

- What is the purpose of the information? ("Objectivity," 2012, para. 1).
- "Is any sponsorship or underwiting fully disclosed?" ("Objectivity," 2012, para. 5). Look for a link "to a page describing the goals or purpose" of the sponsor (Alexander & Tate, 2009f, section b).
- Does the purpose of the Web site help inform you about the reliability of what you are reading?
- Was the resource created to inform, explain, persuade, or for some other purpose?
- What facts are provided and what information appears to be missing? ("Evaluating Web," 2007).
- "If there is any advertising on the page, is it clearly differentiated from the informational content?" (Alexander & Tate, 2009f, section c).
- "If the site relates to a controversial topic, are different sides of the argument represented evenly? When different viewpoints are evenly represented, the site can be considered unbiased or *balanced*, when they are not, the page is biased" ("Evaluating the Objectivity," 2012, para. 3).
- What is the tone of the information? "Good information sources will use a calm, reasoned tone to present information in a balanced manner. . . Writing that is overly critical, attacking, or spiteful often indicates an irrational and unfair presentation rather than a reasoned argument" (Alexander & Tate, 2009f, section a, para. 4).

Sometimes a domain name may be helpful in examining potential bias or slant of information from a source. "For example, the benefits of a new drug might be more objective coming from a government Web site (*.gov*), such as the Food and Drug Administration, rather than those offered by its manufacturer, Bristol-Myers Squibb (*.com*)" (Alexander & Tate, 2009f, section a, para. 3).

## Currency

Generally speaking a writer wants to find the most recent information on a topic. In evaluating a source, ask:

- Is the information up-to-date or has new information on the same subject been published (or placed on the Web) since this resource was made available?

- Is there information available about the most recent update and when it occurred? ("Currency," 2012, para. 1, 2).

Look at the publication date and compare it with your other resources. Occasionally, you will find print resources that do not give a date. This is particularly true of pamphlets and brochures; it is sometimes true of books.

Determining currency of *Web resources* may be more difficult than for print sources as Web authors and Web sites do not always provide the copyright date or the date of the last update. Additionally, with Web resources, you should consider the following (if available):

- When was the document first written?
- When was the document placed on the Web?
- When was last revision of the document? Revisions of Web sites indicate if the site is being maintained.
- Are the Web site's links up to date? (Alexander & Tate, 2009e; "Teaching Students," 1997)

Date of creation, date of placement on the Web, and the revision date usually are found on the home page (generally at the bottom). Some Web sites have links to copyright information. Sometimes each subtopic will have different dates; these dates (creation, placement, or revision) usually will be found at the end of the subtopic page.

## Coverage

In both print and Web sources, information may be presented as a full report or as an excerpt, abstract, or summary. Excerpts, abstracts, and summaries are all incomplete or short versions of the original work. While you can use each of these to determine whether to read the original source, it is generally not a good idea to rely on excerpts, abstracts, and summaries on their own (Hacker & Sommers, 2011, p. 352). The complete written work will provide you with the fullest perspective or discussion of the author's topic and with a number of directions to take in your writing.

Sources themselves vary in how thoroughly a particular subject is discussed. When considering how much depth or coverage exists in a particular source, several questions can be asked:

- "Does the information directly relate to the specific topic?" ("Evaluating the Coverage," 2012, para. 1)
- What topics are included in this resource?
- How much detail has been included?
- Are the topics discussed in depth? (Alexander & Tate, 2009d)
- Is the topic "successfully addressed, with clearly presented arguments and adequate support to substantiate them"? (Alexander & Tate, 2009d, section a).
- Who is the audience? (Alexander & Tate, 2009d)
- Does the source provide updated information?
- Does the source substantiate another source?
- Does the source provide new information?

- Is the information primary or secondary? Primary sources are first-hand reports and original documents. Secondary sources are written using primary sources and are subject to the author's interpretation (Engle, 2013).

## Additional Considerations for Web Resources

Remember that Internet sites are made by a wide variety of individuals and sponsoring institutions or entities. The content ranges from the definitive to the incorrect. Not all sites will be useful; some may bias your project ("Teaching Students," 1997). Also, sometimes the sources used by an author are not specified, making the site you are using hard to evaluate.

Sometimes it is difficult to separate information from advertisements. You will want to consider who is the supplier of the information. If the information is supplied by a commercial firm, it may be biased (Alexander & Tate, 2009f, section c).

### Web links

Most Web resources provide the user with links to other sources. The quality of these links may vary greatly. Learn to be critical of each new Web resource (Alexander & Tate, 2009f, section b). A Web site that is not fully functional or has poor links is an indicator of poor quality.

Here are some questions you may wish to ask about the links:

- "Is there a link at the top or bottom of the page linking back to information about the website's publisher or sponsor?" ("Publisher or," 2005, bullet 2).
- Does there appear to be any link selection criteria, and if yes, what are they?
- "If there are links to other pages as sources, are they to reliable sources?" ("Evaluating Web," 2012, "4.What do others say?", para. 4).
- "Are the links (if any) evaluated and do they complement the documents' themes?" ("Five Criteria," 2010, "5. Coverage of the Web Documents," bullet 1).
- "How up-to-date are the links?" ("Five Criteria," 2010, "4. Currency of Web Documents," bullet 3).
- "How many dead links are on the page?" ("Five Criteria," 2010, "4. Currency of Web Documents," bullet 4).

### Using search engines

When you use a search engine, it generally retrieves Web information out of context. For example, if you used the key words "clothing, historic" the search engine might provide Web citations for museums, living history sites, individuals interested in historical clothing, and members of the Society for Creative Anachronism. The information on historic clothing provided by these sites is very different in content, depth, and reliability. No matter the subject, for each Web source, go to the home page as part of the evaluation of the source and before using the source (Alexander & Tate, 2009c).

### Evaluating Web blogs

Blogs should be evaluated like all other Web sources; consider accuracy, authority, objectivity, currency, and coverage when you evaluate a blog and blogger. Be aware that the individual blog posting can be authored by more than one individual, and blogs may contain advertising. A blog is considered fairly reliable if it links to other writers with whom the authors disagree (Clemmit, 2008). Consider the following:

- "How sophisticated is the language and the spelling?" (Borin & Wolf, 2012, slide 7). [accuracy]
- "Does the blog include hypertext links leading to reputable sources of information?" (Borin & Wolf, 2012, slide 5). [accuracy]
- Does the author have expertise on the issue being discussed? [authority]
    - Does the author provide an easily accessible biography?
    - "Does [the] biography pertain to the subject?" (Freedman, 2010, para. 4).
    - "Are the blog posts signed by an identifiable author?" (Borin & Wolf, 2012, slide 5).
- "Is the content covered in any depth?" ("Evaluating Blogs," 2013, "Evaluating Blogs," bullet 4).
- "Does the blog contain reasonable and rational language, a reserved tone, as well as explanations, definitions, clarifications?" (Borin & Wolf, 2012, slide 7). [objectivity]
- "Is the blog upfront about its bias? Is the blog author tolerant of opposing points of view, recognizing other points of view" (Borin & Wolf, 2012, slide 6).
- "Is this blog alive, containing current and regular posts from the author?" (Borin & Wolf, 2012, slide 6). [currency]
- "Is the blog updated on a regular basis?" (Freedman, 2010, para. 7).
- "Does the blog have a professional appearance?" (Borin & Wolf, 2012, slide 8).

### Last thoughts

Be critical of all resources but especially of Web sources. These sources can be produce by anyone and can have deliberate or accidental alteration. If you have not yet asked a reference librarian to help you find information on your topic, now would be the time to do so. The librarian can help you find other print and non-print resources on your topic.

For additional information on evaluating Web sites, you can Google "Evaluating Web Resources" and look for URL's that contain "edu." Also, check the appendix of this guide for several useful Web sites.

## Additional Considerations for All Resources

Do not rely on a few sources. Whether you are using print or Web resources, *no one author is infallible.* Information changes over time, by discipline, and by interpretation. Your information and final project will be more complete the more sources you use (within your given time limits). Use all of your sources as a means of evaluating each source. However, do not reject an author solely because they present different ideas. Do learn to consider the authors' credentials before making judgments on their work.

*Endnotes*

1. Note: depending on the purpose of your work, some of these criteria will be more important than others. You will want to determine what are the most important evaluation criteria for possible sources before beginning your search for sources.
2. There will be some variation depending on the type of scholarly article. Articles that are themselves primarily a review of literature may or may not have a formal methods section. Similarly, articles that focus on history and sometimes on culture(s) may or may not have a formal methods section. If you are unsure of the quality of a source, ask your instructor.
3. Note: These URL indicators (i.e., .edu, .gov) may change in the near future thus making it more difficult to determine the organization behind a Web site.

# WWW Writing and Style Resources

## WWW Writing Resources

Citation tools. (2013). University Libraries, Kent State University. Retrieved at http://libguides.library.kent.edu/content.php?pid=357387&sid=2945734

Citing information. (2011). University Libraries, University of North Carolina. Retrieved at http://www.lib.unc.edu/instruct/citations/

Handouts. (2010–2012). The Writing Center, University of North Carolina at Chapel Hill. Retrieved from http://writingcenter.unc.edu/handouts/

Plagiarism. (2010–2012). The Writing Center, University of North Carolina at Chapel Hill. Retrieved from http://writingcenter.unc.edu/handouts/plagiarism/

Purdue Online Writing Lab. (1995–2013). *Research and citation resources*. Retrieved from Purdue University Online Writing Lab web site: http://owl.english.purdue.edu/owl/section/2/

Duke University Libraries. (2012). *Research Guide*. Retrieved from http://library.duke.edu/services/instruction/libraryguide/

Writing Intensive Curriculum Program. (2013). *WIC survival guide:* Chapter 1: Writing to learn. Retrieved from the Oregon State University web site: http://wic.oregonstate.edu/writing-learn[1]

## APA Style Checklists

APA style checklist—6th edition. (n.d.). Retrieved from the Valdosta State University web site: http://mypages.valdosta.edu/mwhatley/3600/apachck.pdf

Sullivan University Learning Resource Center. (2013). Checklist for APA 6 style. Retrieved from the Sullivan University web site: http://libguides.sullivan.edu/content.php?pid=289203&sid=2377385

Off Campus Library Services. (2011). APA style check list. Retrieved from: http://www2.indwes.edu/ocls/apa/apastylechecklist.pdf

Wesley College Writing Center. (2010). APA Style Checklist. Retrieved from the Wesley College web site: http://www.wesley.edu/fileadmin/editors_images/Academics/Dept._Academic_Resources/Writing_Handouts/Using_APA_Style_in_Writing/APA_Style_Checklist.pdf

## Evaluating WWW Resources

Alexander, J., & Tate, M. (2009). *Evaluating internet sources: A library resource guide*. Lydia M. Olson Library. Retrieved from the Northern Michigan University web site: http://library.nmu.edu/guides/userguides/webeval.htm

Borin, J., & Wolf, M. (2012). *How to evaluate blogs* [PowerPoint Presentation]. Retrieved from the Widener University web site: http://www.widener.edu/about/campus_resources/wolfgram_library/evaluate/blogs.aspx

Evaluating web content: Blogs and wikis. (n.d.). University Libraries. Retrieved from the University of Albany, State University of New York web site: http://librvary.albany.edu/usered/eval/evalweb/blogswikis.html

Evaluating web sites and blogs. (2013). School of Law Library. Retrieved from the University of Akron web site: http://law.uakron.libguides.com/evaluating_websites

Evaluating web sites: Criteria and tools. (2012). Olin & Uris Libraries. Retrieved from the Cornell University Library web site: http://olinuris.library.cornell.edu/ref/research/webeval.html

Freedman, T. (2010). 10 ways to evaluate blogs. The Educational Technology Site. Retrieved from: http://www.ictineducation.org/home-page/2010/8/19/10-ways-to-evaluate-blogs.html

Note: Web addresses may have changed since the printing of this manual.

### *Endnote*

1. Subsequent *WIC Survival Guide* chapters can be accessed from this URL.

# References


Accuracy. (2012). *Criteria for evaluating web resources.* University Libraries. Retrieved from the Kent State University web site: http://www.library.kent.edu/page/10475

Agins, T. (1999). *The end of fashion: How marketing changed the clothing business forever.* New York, NY: HarperCollins.

Alexander, J., & Tate, M. (2009a). *Evaluating internet sources: A library resource guide.* Lydia M. Olson Library. Retrieved from the Northern Michigan University web site: http://library.nmu.edu/guides/userguides/webeval.htm

Alexander, J., & Tate, M. (2009b). Accuracy. *Evaluating internet sources: A library resource guide.* Lydia M. Olson Library. Retrieved from the Northern Michigan University web site: http://library.nmu.edu/guides/userguides/webeval.htm

Alexander, J., & Tate, M. (2009c). Authority. *Evaluating internet sources: A library resource guide.* Lydia M. Olson Library. Retrieved from the Northern Michigan University web site: http://library.nmu.edu/guides/userguides/webeval.htm

Alexander, J., & Tate, M. (2009d). Coverage. *Evaluating internet sources: A library resource guide.* Lydia M. Olson Library. Retrieved from the Northern Michigan University web site: http://library.nmu.edu/guides/userguides/webeval.htm

Alexander, J., & Tate, M. (2009e). Currency. *Evaluating internet sources: A library resource guide.* Lydia M. Olson Library. Retrieved from the Northern Michigan University web site: http://library.nmu.edu/guides/userguides/webeval.htm

Alexander, J., & Tate, M. (2009f). Objectivity. *Evaluating internet sources: A library resource guide.* Lydia M. Olson Library. Retrieved from the Northern Michigan University web site: http://library.nmu.edu/guides/userguides/webeval.htm

Authority. (2012). *Criteria for evaluating web resources.* University Libraries. Retrieved from the Kent State University web site: http://www.library.kent.edu/page/10475

Authority. (2013). *Checklist for evaluating web resources.* USM Libraries. Retrieved from the University of Southern Maine web site: http://usm.maine.edu/library/checklist-evaluating-web-resources

Authorship and affiliations. (1995–2013). *Evaluating print vs. internet sources.* OWL Purdue Online Writing Lab. Retrieved from Purdue University web site: http://owl.english.purdue.edu/owl/resource/553/04/

Borin, J., & Wolf, M. (2012). How to evaluate blogs [PowerPoint presentation]. Retrieved from the Widener University web site: http://www.widener.edu/about/campus_resources/wolfgram_library/evaluate/blogs.aspx

Breward, C. (1995). *The culture of fashion: A new history of fashionable dress.* Manchester, Great Britain: Manchester University Press.

Brogan, P. F. (1977). *East of the Cascades.* Portland, OR: Binford & Mort, Publishers.

Carmichael, E., & Farrell, H. (2012). Evaluation of the effectiveness of online resources in developing student critical thinking: Review of literature and case study of a critical thinking online site. *Journal of University Teaching & Learning Practice, 9*(1), Article 4. Retrieved from: http://ro.uow.edu.au/cgi/viewcontent.cgi?article=1246&context=jutlp

Chenoune, F. (1993). *A history of men's fashion* (D. Dusinberre, Trans.). Paris, France: Flammarion.

Clemmit, M. (2008, August 1). Internet accuracy: The issues. *CQ Researcher, 18*(27), 627–634.

Consequences of plagiarism. (n.d.). *Learning Resources Center.* Retrieved from Strayer University web site: https://icampus.strayer.edu/lrc/plagiarism/consequences

Currency. (2012). *Criteria for evaluating web resources.* University Libraries. Retrieved from the Kent State University web site: http://www.library.kent.edu/page/10475

DK Publishing, Inc. (1998). *DK illustrated Oxford dictionary.* London, Great Britain: Author.

*The domestic architecture of England during the Tudor period: Illustrated in a series of photographs and measured drawings of country mansions and manor houses, with details.* (1923). Boston, MA: s.n. [1]

Engle, M. (2013). Critically analyzing information sources. Retrieved from Cornell University Library web site: http://guides.library.cornell.edu/print_content.php?pid=318835&sid=2612843&mode=g

Evaluating blogs. (2013). *Evaluating web resources.* Retrieved from the Berry College Memorial Library web site: http://libguides.berry.edu/content.php?pid=190975&sid=1601959

Evaluating the coverage of web sites. (2012). Information Literacy Tutorial. Retrieved from the State University of New York, Jefferson web site: http://sunyjefferson.libguides.com/content.php?pid=127609&sid=1115781

Evaluating the objectivity of web sites. (2012). Information Literacy Tutorial. Retrieved from the State University of New York, Jefferson web site: http://sunyjefferson.libguides.com/content.php?pid=127609&sid=1115769

Evaluating web pages. (2007). *Research guide.* Retrieved from the Duke University Libraries web site: http://library.duke.edu/services/instruction/libraryguide/evalwebpages.html#objectivity

Evaluating web pages: Techniques to apply & questions to ask. (2012). *Finding information on the internet: A tutorial.* Retrieved from Teaching Library Internet Workshops, University of California Berkeley web site: http://www.lib.berkeley.edu/TeachingLib/Guides/Internet/Evaluate.html

Felder, R. M., & Soloman, B. A. (n.d.). *Learning styles and strategies.* Retrieved from http://www4.ncsu.edu/unity/lockers/users/f/felder/public/ILSdir/styles.htm

Five criteria for evaluating web pages. (2010). Retrieved from Olin & Uris Libraries, Cornell University Library web site: http://olinuris.library.cornell.edu/ref/research/webcrit.html

Fleming, N. D., & Mills, C. (1992). Not another inventory, rather a catalyst for reflections. *To Improve the Academy, 11*, 137–155.

Freedman, T. (2010). *10 ways to evaluate blogs.* The Educational Technology site. Retrieved from http://www.ictineducation.org/home-page/2010/8/19/10-ways-to-evaluate-blogs.html

Glock, R. E., & Kunz, G. I. (2000). *Apparel manufacturing sewn product analysis* (3rd ed.). Upper Saddle River, NJ: Prentice Hall.

Hacker, D., & Sommers, N. (2011). *A writer's reference* (7th ed.). Boston, MA: Bedford/St. Martin's.

Haisley, T. (2002, February). Brooks Brothers digital tailors measure up. *Bobbin*, 26–30.

Harris, R. (2010, November 22). Evaluating Internet research sources. Virtual Salt. Retrieved from http://www.virtualsalt.com/evalu8it.htm

In-Text Citations: Author/Authors. (1995–2013). The Writing Lab & The OWL at Purdue. Retrieved from Purdue University web site: http://owl.english.purdue.edu/owl/resource/560/03/

Johnson, M. J., & Moore, E. C. (2001). *Apparel product development* (2nd ed.). Upper Saddle River, NJ: Prentice Hall.

Jones, R. C. (2013, July 29). The instructor's challenge: Moving students beyond opinions to critical thinking. *Faculty Focus*, [eZine]. Retrieved from http://www.facultyfocus.com/articles/effective-teaching-strategies/the-instructors-challenge-moving-students-beyond-opinions-to-critical-thinking/

Kidwell, C. B., & Christman, M. C. (1974). *Suiting everyone: The democratization of clothing in America.* Washington D.C.: Smithsonian Institution Press.

Lee, C. (2009, October 23). How to cite Twitter and Facebook, Part 1: General. *APA Style* [web log]. Retrieved from http://blog.apastyle.org/apastyle/2009/10/how-to-cite-twitter-and-facebook-part-i.html

Lee, C. (2009, October 26). How to cite Twitter and Facebook, Part II: Reference list entries and in-text citations [web log]. Retrieved from http://blog.apastyle.org/apastyle/2009/10/how-to-cite-twitter-and-facebook-part-ii.html

Lehnert, G. (1998). *Fashion: An illustrated historical overview*. Hauppauge, NY: Barrons.

McKowen, C. (1996). *Get your A out of college* (rev. ed.). Menlo Park, CA: Crisp Publications Inc.

Moffett, M. Fazio, M., & Wodehouse, L. (2004). *A world history of architecture*. Boston, MA: McGraw Hill.

Objectivity. (2012). *Criteria for evaluating web resources*. University Libraries. Retrieved from the Kent State University web site: http://www.library.kent.edu/page/10475

Plagiarism. (2010–2012). The Writing Center, University of North Carolina at Chapel Hill. Retrieved from http://writingcenter.unc.edu/handouts/plagiarism/

Prown, J. D. (1993). The truth of material culture: History or fiction? In S. Lubar & W. D. Kingery (Eds.). *History from things: Essay on material culture* (pp. 1–19). Washington, D.C.: Smithsonian.

*Publication manual of the American Psychological Association* (6th ed.). (2010). Washington D.C.: American Psychological Association.

Publisher or sponsor. (2005). *Evaluating web information*. Retrieved from Information Literacy Instruction, The University of North Carolina Asheville web site: http://www.lib.unca.edu/library/lr/evalweb.html

Robinson, F. (1970). *Effective study*. New York, NY: Harper & Row.

Scope. (2013). *Checklist for evaluating web resources*. USM Libraries. Retrieved from the University of Southern Maine web site: http://usm.maine.edu/library/checklist-evaluating-web-resources

Sproles, G. B., & Burns, L. D. (1994). *Changing appearances: Understanding dress in contemporary society*. New York, NY: Fairchild.

State & County QuickFacts: Oregon. (2013). United States Census Bureau, U.S. Department of Commerce. Retrieved from http://quickfacts.census.gov/qfd/states/41000.html.

Storey, W. K. (1999). *Writing history: A guide for students*. New York, NY: Oxford University Press.

Successful students: Guidelines and thoughts for academic success. (1996). *The Teaching Professor, 10*(9), 2.

Sutton, I. (1999). *Western architecture*. New York, NY: Thames and Hudson.

Teaching students to evaluate internet sites. (1997). *The Teaching Professor, 11*(7), 4.

Test-taking strategies. (2011). *The basics of effective learning*. Retrieved from the Bucks County Community College web site: http://faculty.bucks.edu/specpop/tests.htm

Three learning styles. (2002–2010). Academic Enrichment, Bepko Learning Center. Retrieved from Indiana University web site: http://blc.uc.iupui.edu/AcademicEnrichment/StudySkills/LearningStyles/3LearningStyles.aspx

Tortora, P. G., & Eubank, K. (2010). *Survey of historic costume: A history of western dress* (5th ed.). New York, NY: Fairchild Books.

Van Bramer, S. E. (1995). What is plagiarism. Retrieved from http://science.widener.edu/svb/essay/plagiar.html

Weinstein, C. E. (1994). Students at risk for academic failure: Learning to learn classes. In K. W. Prichard & R. M. Sawyer (Eds.). *Handbook of college teaching: Theory and applications* (pp. 375–385). Westport, CT: Greenwood Press.

What's your learning style? (2009). Retrieved from: http://www.sunburst.usd.edu/~bwjames/tut/Learning-style/

Who is the web site's author? (2013). *Evaluating web resources*. University of Maryland University College. Retrieved from: http://www.umuc.edu/library/libhow/webresources.cfm

Why do we reference? (2013). Language and Learning Online, Monash University. Retrieved from: http://monash.edu/lls/llonline/writing/general/reference/index.xml

## *Endnote*

1. Notice there is no publisher listed in this reference; instead you have the letters "s.n." This is a fairly rare occurrence but it signifies that no publisher was identified with the book. These letters, "s.n.," stand for a latin term, *sine nomine*. This means the publisher is unknown, unlisted, or not printed.